Francis Green

Vox oculis subjecta

A dissertation on the most curious and important art of imparting speech and the

knowledge of language

Francis Green

Vox oculis subjecta
A dissertation on the most curious and important art of imparting speech and the knowledge of language

ISBN/EAN: 9783337257941

Printed in Europe, USA, Canada, Australia, Japan

Cover: Foto ©Paul-Georg Meister /pixelio.de

More available books at **www.hansebooks.com**

"VOX OCULIS SUBJECTA;"

A

DISSERTATION

ON THE

Moſt *Curious* and Important Art of

Imparting SPEECH, and the Knowledge of LANGUAGE, to the *naturally* DEAF, and (conſequently) DUMB;

With a particular Account of

The ACADEMY of Meſſrs. BRAIDWOOD of Edinburgh,

AND

A PROPOSAL

To perpetuate, and extend the Benefits thereof.

" Per varios uſus *artem experientia* fecit,
" Exemplo monſtrante viam." —

By a PARENT.

LONDON:

Sold by BENJAMIN WHITE, N° 63, Fleet-ſtreet.

MDCCLXXXIII.

PREFACE.

POLITICKS and party views, which, at this day, occupy and engross the minds of so many, have no place or share in this unambitious publication; of course prejudices and resentments, on that ground, cannot be provoked.

A great part of this essay being obviously either *compilation, and quotation, or narrative*; it must necessarily be apparent, that literary fame cannot be its object.

It is neither an attempt at composition, nor at criticism; but, without ostentation, hath its origin in the *simple* principles of sympathy and philanthropy.

The primary motive is, an ardent folicitude that the benefits of an ingenious method *(new* in *extenſive* practice, if not new in theory) of infinite importance to many individuals, may be univerſally realized:— Having myſelf *collaterally* experienced the ineffable ſatisfaction conſequent on its practicability, I am urged by an impatience kindled by ſocial affection, to communicate the conſolation to *all* others who may *ever* be in the ſame predicament.

This, although a ſecondary, is not a ſmall inducement.

The Editor is not unapprized, that ſeveral treatiſes have been publiſhed on this art, *in the laſt century,* by men of diſtinction in the literary world, viz. Dr. *Amman* of Amſterdam, Dr. *John Wallis,* and Dr. *William Holder* (by the two former in *Latin):*

Latin): and also by *Bulwer* in English. They are *all*, now, become rare books, and hardly to be met with, as he hath experienced.---The subject is also touched upon in a late Essay, intitled Elements of Speech, by *J. Herries*, A. M. 1773.— Extracts from, or translations of particular parts of each, are inserted in the body of this; but neither of them had *altogether* the same grounds, nor the same points in view with this : Nor did they flow from the feelings of a parent.

That an art tending effectually to rescue a *certain proportion* of the human species in every age, and in every country, from *idleness, ignorance,* and *wretchedness,* may be perpetuated, and its benefits happily extended to every possible subject, is (it is conceived) of no trifling consequence to society, collectively :—To those who are or may

may be *born* deaf, especially, and their immediate connexions, it must be deemed invaluable.

If the cultivation of the human mind be the pursuit and end of philosophy, if the salvation of the soul be the use, object, and glory of theology, divines and philosophers will, at least, give credit for the intention, which is always the best apology for the most indifferent performance.

To convince *the world* of the practicability of this extraordinary art *(incredible to many)*, and to endeavour to prevent its being lost, like many other arts, after having been brought to perfection; to excite the attention of the public to a plan, which (if the rational nature is superior to the animal) hath objects the most interesting and affecting, is the ultimate design of

PREFACE.

this publication:—Should this prove the means of *one* only of the human race, in whom " *the particle of the divinity*" is inhærent, being raifed from an humiliating, moſt melancholy ſtate by nature, and added to the number of *converſible* and *happy* intellectual beings, not only the application it hath coſt will be abundantly compenſated for, but the hours expended herein will ever be confidered amongſt the moſt uſefully employed, as well as the moſt important and valuable of thoſe beſtowed by Providence, upon

March,
1783.

The AUTHOR.

ERRATA.

P. xiv. (Contents) l. 13. *dele* end.
P. 23. l. 9. *for* effect, *r.* defect.
P. 25. l. 14. *for* was, *r.* is.
P. 36. l. ult. *for* are, *r.* is.
P. 68. l. 12. *r.* " and of the *instruments* of *voice* and
    " *articulation.*"
P. 94. l. 17. *r. not* to be thought on.
P. 101. l. ult. *dele* doth.
P. 128. l. 7. *for* throughout, *r.* thoroughly.
P. 137. l. ult. *for* naso-dental, *r.* naso-vocal.
P. 184. l. 1, 2. *r.* direction and authority.
P. 159. l. 17. *for* remarkable, *r.* remarkably.

CONTENTS.

INTRODUCTION.

The natural *disposition* of mankind for conversation, and intercourse of mind.

Man endued with capacities by nature,—many of his faculties are not *natural*, but acquired.—Nothing valuable attained without perseverance of exertions.—Language a special instance.

Reason, as well as *social affection*, interwoven in our nature;—in the dumb both are fully apparent.—Speech necessary to bring them into exercise, and improve them.—Use and value of language.

PART

CONTENTS.
PART I.

Picture of the melancholy state of such as are born *deaf,* or lose their hearing in infancy, and who remain *deaf and dumb.*

Relief effectually pointed out by Providence; the means well known to *a few,* but not universally known.—The art invented, and partially practised, in the last century.

The cause of want of speech, or deprivation of language (generally) is deafness.—Summary description of the ear.—No other want of capacity (usually) in dumb persons.

Review of capacities, compared with man's capacity in general.—*Powers of mind, voice, and organs of speech.*—The practicability of imparting speech, so that they may understand and use it, by alteration of perception from the auditory to the optic nerve.—The sounds of words arbitrary, as well as the form.

From

Form discernible by the eye; utterance may be learnt by *feeling* and *seeing*.

No universal *system* of articulate language;—Plausible objection. Objection obviated.—Probable original state of human nature.—First substitutes for language, exemplified in several nations or savage *tribes*.—Cursory description of articulation.—Natural language nothing more than the vocal tones, with signs, and expessions of the countenance.—This *only natural* language may be methodized into a practicable system by *all persons* possessed of *understanding*, and the *instruments* of *voice* and *articulation*, consequently by the deaf.—Hint of the mode.

Extracts and quotations from authors who have *formerly* treated of the *theory* and *practice* of this art.

PART

PART II.

Particular account of the Academy of *Meſſrs. Braidwood* of Edinburgh;—a great philoſophical curioſity.—Relation of the progreſs of *a ſon* at that Academy. Reflexions on the contraſt between the cutivated ſtate of the deaf, and their former ſtate.—The author's tribute of gratitude and applauſe.

PART III.

Propoſal *to extend*, as well as *perpetuate* the benefits of this important art.
The *ſtate, capacity,* and *numbers* of the objects ſtrong inducements to this end. end.—A charitable fund neceſſary, under the directions of proper governors.—Such an inſtitution likely to meet with encouragement.—The example of the *Royal Bounty.*—The importance to *individuals*

viduals (of a temporal and spiritual nature) and to *society*.—The obligations of humanity to promote the establishment of a charitable institution for the benefit of *indigent* persons, and to perpetuate the *curious* art.—Reflexions on the prevalence of *Dissipation*, and the love of fashionable pleasures over useful schemes.—The *Royal Society* have always encouraged the theory of this art.—They, and the *opulent clergy*, and others, would probably favor a well-directed plan for this purpose.—A source of satisfaction to *all* good men.—The *universal obligation* of benevolence and charity.

APPENDIX.

Extracts from various authors, on the subject of *Messrs. Braidwoods'* Academy, viz.

Mr. Arnot—History of Edinburgh.

Dr. Johnson—Journey to the Hebrides.

Lord Monboddo—Origin and Progress of Language.

Pennant's—Tour through Scotland.

Specimen of the degree of perfection in language to which some of Mr. Braidwood's pupils have attained.

Sketch of a proposed plan.

VOX

"VOX OCULIS SUBJECTA;"

ON

The Curious and Important Art of imparting Language to the Deaf.

INTRODUCTION.

MAN, as a social being, hath an irresistible propensity to communicate with his species, to receive the ideas of others, and to impart his own conceptions: this natural disposition for society and conversation is very early apparent in infancy, and as " Nature never gravitates to nought," it hath universally provided the means of

fulfilling

fulfilling its dictates (except perhaps in the comparatively few instances of ideots); that is, it hath bestowed *capacities*, for gradually acquiring all such habits and faculties as are requisite and convenient to us, or conducive to its own purposes. In some, those natural *capacities* or capabilities are complete, in others partial; but, *in all*, they require, like every species of soil, cultivation and improvement.

That mankind are designed for a state of *active* intercourse, seems evident from this consideration alone, that every acquisition is progressive, and very little of our knowledge is from intuition. Even our most common faculties, although acquired by insensible degrees, are the effect of habit. Every great and valuable end is attainable only by slow degrees: no

art

art or science was ever brought to perfection on a sudden.

Nothing exemplifies this position more incontestibly than *language*, emphatically and elegantly defined, " The joint energy " of our best and noblest faculties, reason " and social affection *."

The seeds or elements of reason and social affection are connate with us, and inseparable from our constitution as intellectual beings; they spring up, bud, blossom, and bear fruit in *due season*, in proportion to the culture and manure they receive: they manifest themselves *even in those who have never enjoyed the means and advantages of attaining speech,* as absolutely, (though not so copiously,) as in other men:—the operations of *their* minds in many instances

* Harris's Hermes.

are demonstrated beyond the possibility of a doubt (although inexpressible by them *in words*); but, as the pathetic poet, in painting the blessings of language, and the reciprocal enjoyments of conversation and friendship, says,

Tis " SPEECH, that ventilates our intellec-
   " tual fires."
   ———" Thoughts shut up want air,
" And spoil, like bales unopen'd to the
   " sun.—
" Had thought been all, sweet *speech* had
   " been deny'd;
" *Speech, thought's canal! Speech, thought's*
   " *criterion too!*
" Thought in the mine may come forth
   " gold or dross;
" When coin'd in words, we know its real
   " worth.
                              " Thought,

" VOX OCULIS SUBJECTA."

> " Thought, too, deliver'd, is the more pof-
> " feſt;
> " Teaching, we learn; and, giving, we re-
> " tain
> " The births of intellect;—when dumb
> " forgot."   " Young."

The uſe, advantage and neceſſity of ſpeech, or *articulate language, to every individual in a ſtate of ſociety*, are ſo exceedingly obvious and ſtriking, that any farther attempt to illuſtrate them cannot but be ſuperfluous. In every ſtation and condition of life, tranſactions muſt ariſe, *even from our natural wants*, to which, without this faculty, we ſhould in a great degree be incompetent. What purpoſe then more worthy of humanity than that of providing a remedy for a defect in *many* of our own ſpecies, which is ſo eſſential an obſtruction to their happineſs?

PART I.

DISSERTATION

ON

The Curious and Important Art of imparting LANGUAGE to the DEAF.

THE catalogue of infirmities and calamities to which human nature is subject, exhibits, perhaps, no case of our fellow-creatures (insanity of mind excepted) that more forcibly, or more justly, excites our commiseration, than that of the *deaf and dumb*.

"No corporeal defect," says a late author on the Elements of Speech, "renders an individual so *uncomfortable* to *himself* and *others* as that of *deafness*.—

"*Not*

8 "VOX OCULIS SUBJECTA."

"*Not even those who are blind* are half so
"*pitiable:* they are generally social and
"lively: the pleasures of conversation,
"the *charms* of music, supply the want of
"the other sense.—It is true, we re-
"ceive an inexpressible delight in survey-
"ing the various productions of nature
"and art: yet still the pleasure is more
"selfish and confined, than that which re-
"sults from the objects of hearing and the
"exercise of the vocal powers."—"How
"dull and solitary appear the men who
"are *deaf* and *speechless!*"

The principal channel through which
instruction and knowledge (the sources
of infinite pleasure) are usually conveyed
to the mind, is the ear. This, by some
internal, unaccountable misformation, or
derangement (of *their* organs of hearing,)
is blocked up for ever! to *them,* all na-

ture wears a solemn silence; the consequence is, that speech, that mark of humanity, that peculiar ornament and dignity, which chiefly distinguishes man from the brute creation, is unattainable in the *common* way, it being, evidently, by the imitation of the sounds which *we hear*, that mankind *ordinarily* acquire the art, or the faculty of speech.—In the midst of multitudes, *they* may be said to be in solitude.

Whenever we meet a person (although an entire stranger) in this unhappy predicament, or reflect on the melancholy situation of such as were born *deaf*, and remain (consequently) *dumb*, does not our sensibility receive a shock, which is too violent and complicated to admit of description?—Excluded from the knowledge of every thing, except the *immediate* objects of sense, apparently doomed to ignorance, idleness,

idleneſs, and uſeleſſneſs, a burden to their friends and to ſociety, incapable in ſuch a ſtate of that ſocial intercourſe and communication of mind, which conſtitute the moſt pleaſing and rational enjoyment of intellectual beings, without diſtinct ideas of moral obligation, of their duty to God, or the nature and end of their exiſtence; what pitiable animals are men, in ſuch circumſtances, and how little ſuperior to the brutes!

The mind flies off with pain, if not with horror, from the affecting idea.

After the conſideration of their deplorable caſe, what pleaſure muſt the benevolent heart receive from the information, that, whatever may have been the former fate of ſuch perſons, *all ſuch* may now be reſcued from their miſerable condition, and enabled

enabled to become not only *happy* and *useful*, but even *learned* members of society; for Providence, in infinite mercy, hath been pleased to point out a method, by which they may be taught, *in effect to hear*, and *in reality to speak and read*; to attain such a perfect knowledge of language, as (by observing the motion of the mouth in others) to *converse* intelligibly *viva voce*; to express their own sentiments not only distinctly, but elegantly in writing, and even, in process of time, to translate one language into another; consequently to learn arithmetic, geography, mathematics, and any other art, or science (practical music excepted): but, above all, to have a thorough knowledge of the *dignifying* principles of *morality* and vital *religion*. That this fact, however astonishing, is well known to many, (although not so universally as is hoped it will be) several respectabe spectable characters have some time ago testified to the world, in the newspapers and magazines. Among the many who have attended the public examination, and attested the progress of several pupils of the justly celebrated Mr. *Braidwood* of Edinburgh, (who hath brought this very curious, *important*, and almost incredible art to a much greater degree of perfection than any former professor) were the late Lord *Morton*, President of the Royal Society, Lord *Hales*, Doctor *Robertson*, Sir *John Pringle*, Doctor *Franklin*, and Doctor *Hunter*, &c.

The following authors have also incontestibly confirmed the information, viz. Mr. *Arnot*, in his History of Edinburgh; Dr. *Johnson*, in his Tour through Scotland to the Hebrides; Mr. *Pennant*, in his Tour through ditto; Lord *Monboddo*,

in

in his Origin and Progress of Language *.

It is remarkable (notwithstanding all that had been written by *Plato, Aristotle, Dionisius* the Halicarnassian, *Quinctilian,* and others of the antients, who have investigated the principles of language and the formation of the vocal and articulate sounds) that until about the middle of the last century, we know of no *attempts* having been made in *this extraordinary art,* and at that time in only a few instances; it existed then indeed *chiefly* in theory; there were, however, some instances of succefsful practice. *Bullwer* relates, in his Philocophus, or Deaf and Dumb Man's Friend, published

---

* Extracts from each author are hereunto subjoined in the Appendix, in order to comprize, as it were in one view, such corroboration of the account herein given, as to leave (I hope) no doubt in the minds of any into whose hands this may chance to fall.

in 1648, an instance of a Spanish nobleman instructed by a priest. Dr. *W. Holder* taught *one* young gentleman in this country, to make some proficiency in 1659—Doctor *John Wallis,* Fellow of the Royal Society, and Savilian Professor of Geometry at *Oxford,* instructed *two* in some degree, about the year 1660.

The ingenious Doctor *John Amman* of *Amsterdam* also instructed a young lady at *Haerlem,* and several others in Holland, between the years 1690 and 1700—Some attempts had been made also by *Van Helmont,* a German, and by *Monachus,* a Spaniard.

Mr. Baker likewise latterly professed the art in this country, and practised it with some success, about *twenty-five or thirty years ago;* but no regular academy was ever opened

opened by either.—It was reserved for that *" hot bed of genius"* (Edinburgh) *to bring to maturity* so great a curiosity.

Besides the abovementioned academy, there are *now* others, where the art is taught, not only in England, but in France and Germany; but, as these observations are intended to be made upon the knowledge *personally obtained, from the testimony of the author's own senses*, and as that knowledge is chiefly confined to the school or academy at Edinburgh, where he *now* hath a son, who has made the most satisfactory proficiency, it is meant herein to advert to that academy only, at present governed and instructed by Mess. *Thomas* and *John Braidwood*.

Before we proceed to the relation of facts, let us consider the cause of the want

of

of speech (in those who are *deaf* and *dumb*), and also their natural capacities compared with man's capacity in general; perswaded that a little reflection on those points will be sufficient to convince the most incredulous, that there is *not*, in the nature of things, any physical impossibility, in teaching such to converse intelligibly, as many, *who have not thought* upon the subject, are apt to imagine.

Lest argument, however, should not prove effectual, the testimony of the dead (as well as the living) shall be afterwards produced; and their speculations, too, *in addition* to what shall here be offered on the practicability of this wonderful art.

The dumb *(in general)* are not so from a deficiency in the organs of speech; the sole cause of their misfortune is a deviation

tion of nature, in the construction of that intricate and most unintelligible part of the human frame, *the organs of hearing.* This part is acknowledged by all anatomists to be so complicated, so prodigiously nice in its formation, that their knowledge of its nature, of the peculiar uses of the respective component particles, and of the operations of sound, are very imperfect, compared with their knowledge of the other parts of our wonderful machine. The result of all their dissections, and their researches into the principles of this sense, and its organs, amounts to little more than ascertaining the positions of the various *internal parts,* viz. the *meatus auditorius,* or auditory passage; the *tympanum;* the *four ossicles,* or small bones, called the *malleus, incus, stapes,* and *orbiculare;* the two apertures called *fenestræ,* two small passages, four muscles, a branch of a nerve, the labyrinth, *perios-*

teum,

team, the *vestible, and auditory nerve*, &c. without being able to agree * in accounting
for

* The following may serve to confirm this assertion: viz.

"Anatomists have *long* disputed, whether the *chorda tympani* was *artery, vein,* or *nerve,* or the *tendon* one of the muscles of the *malleus,* but now discovered to be a branch of the fifth pair of nerves, which meets the *porto dura* of the auditory nerve."
Chambers' Dict. of A. and S.

The labyrinth is supposed by some to contain *innate air.*

"*Schelhammer* denies the *existence* of the *innate* air, so much talked of in the labyrinth, and with good reason, as there is a passage out of the *labyrinth* into the throat, through which the innate air must escape;—this is past doubt, since by stopping the breath, and straining, we can force the external air into the ear, and even hear it rushing in."
Cyclopædia, or Chambers' Dict.—*on the Ear.*

"The tympanum suffers often a *relaxation,* sometimes a *disruption:* if it only lose something of its ancient stretch, it only can receive impressions of great sounds, as of such as first relaxed it; if it be entirely broke, *the hearing is lost:* since the *air* can be no longer *modified* as it ought to be, and is therefore unfit for *moving* or *compressing* the auditory nerve." P. 96.

"The

for the conveyance of the impreſſions of ſound: the auditory nerve is doubtleſs the moſt immediate, eſſential inſtrument of the ſenſe of hearing, but the various avenues to it are ſo marvellouſly intricate, that the moſt minute impediment in either may render it inacceſſible to ſound. The tympanum, or cover to the whole of the *inte-*

"The agitated air occurring with an ear inſinuates itſelf into the *meatus auditorius*, impels the *tympanum*, which being moved, *moves* the "innate air," and the three little bones, and they the auditory nerve." *Beare's Senſorium*, p. 102, publiſhed 1710.

An additional proof of this aſſertion is, that, in 1767, one of Mr. B's naturally deaf pupils having died, and it being ſuppoſed of a dropſy in the head, a diſſection was made, in order to diſcover (if poſſible) the cauſe of the fatal diſorder as well as that of deafneſs—a number of eminent phyſicians and ſurgeons of Edinburgh attended, and could not diſcover any want, or any defect in the parts uſually found in the head.—It would be too tedious to peruſe the *various* differing opinions, from the time of *Hippocrates* and *Galen*, of *Bartholinus, Laurentius, Campanella, Mercurialis, Fabricius Hildanus*, and other remarkable characters of the faculty.

rior ear, is the first portal of admission (if I may so express it) on the due tension and condition of which any further entrance greatly depends; the use of this is, principally, to guard the auditory nerve, brain, and inward parts of the ear, from outward injury by cold, dust, &c. and hath been (not unaptly) compared by some to glass widows, being pervious to sound, as those to light; that this is its *principal* use, hath been proved by experiments upon animals, who, after the tympanum was broken, did not hear the worse for some considerable time, that is, until some other causes, such as cold, impaired the parts within;—but, for passage of sound to the auditory nerve, by which the sense is conveyed to the brain, it is requisite, that this membrane be hard stretched, otherwise the laxness will deaden, or damp the sound;—to preserve this due tension is the use of the *malleus* particularly, which (being fixed to a diftenfible mufcle) ftretches the furface of the tympanum in the centre, and by drawing it inward, transforms it from a plane to a conoid, within the fame circumference; and fo keeps it in due order.—The want of this tenfion, from the misformation, or ftraining of thofe extremely delicate parts, *(oftentimes, no doubt, by the convulfive motions before birth)* is, PERHAPS, the moft frequent caufe of want of hearing (although many caufes are affignable) and it is for this reafon, that fome deaf perfons hear fpeech, a little, when a drum beats near them, or when in a carriage running on pavement (that do not hear at all, at other times;) becaufe the violent percuffion of the air beats in the tympanum to a fuitable degree, as wind fills and expands

the

the sails of a ship, which otherwise hang loose and flaccid.

The causes, however, of deafness, both natural and adventitious, *may be* as various as the numerous, respective minute parts on which hearing depends, and being *internal*, and not to be investigated by sight, it is not always possible to determine precisely where the defect lies, nor indeed, if it were (by reason of its inaccessibleness) to remedy it. Neither is it within the compass of the present design to treat fully * on the sense of hearing; but only to touch upon the subject as far as might be necessary for *some* to understand how easily that part of the bodily system is disordered, and in order to

* For particular information of a modern system, vid. *Differt. de Mr. Geoffray sur l'Organe de l'Oue de l'Homme.*

lead

lead the mind to attend to the important consequences thereof, which are the subject of this attempt.—Be the *cause* of want of hearing, naturally, or by subsequent accident, what it may, the certain *effect* is destitution or privation of the common faculty of speech. Being *dumb* is only the consequence of being *deaf*, not an independent effect, nor owing to any infallible sympathy of the nerves of *hearing* and *those of the tongue*, as Montaigne, and many of the ancients, supposed *. Many have *remained* dumb who were *not born* deaf, but who have lost their hearing in *infancy, before they had acquired* speech; for, indeed, *we are all born dumb*, that is,

---

* "The whole cause of which evil *Platerus* (indeed) imputes to the *sympathetical eague* between the conjugation of nerves, from the auditory nerve propagated to the nerves of the tongues."
Bulwer's Philocophus, p. 122.

speechless, for a time;—the loss of hearing also at any age, will *in time* incur the loss of speech, either totally or partially, of which there are many instances, (several of which are within my own knowledge), of whom some have regained it, by means of the extraordinary art now under our consideration.

The following extracts will be sufficient in support of this truth, and may be necessary for the satisfaction of those to whom it is new.

"*Fabricius Hildanus,*" in his Chirurgical Observations, " speakes of a sonne, of the
" reverend and most excellent man both
" for learning and pietie, *Joannes de l'Ozea,*
" minister of the Moretenfian church,
" whom Hildanus remembers to have been
" a boy very well educated, lively, and for
" his

" his age ſtrong and *talkative*, until about
" the *eighth* yeare of his age; at which
" time being taken with a grievous diſeaſe,
" he was cured rather by the benefit of
" nature than of phyſique: for no rational
" phyſician was called to adminiſter unto
" him preſently after his diſeaſe, when by
" little and little he grew ſo deafe, that he
" *no longer underſtood* what any one ſpake
" unto him: *he became alſo mute*: neither
" could he to this time be reſtored by any
" remedies: he lived when *Hildanus* wrote
" this centurie at *Moratum*, well enough
" married, where he was famous for an ex-
" cellent turner, which is the art he exerciſ-
" eth. *Hildanus* was an eye-witneſſe of
" his conceited and crafty wit, which
" was ſuch that he underſtood the minde
" of thoſe that were converſant with him,
" at the firſt ſight, by the geſture of their
" body: but this muteneſſe happened not
" unto

"unto him through any sympathetical af-
"fection of the tongue with his eare; but
"by a privation of consequence; for being
"at the eighth yeare of his age not suffi-
"ciently confirmed and grounded in his
"mother tongue, hereupon, when he could
"no longer understand what men spoke,
"he easily lost that which he had formerly
"learnt.

"*Platerus* hath somewhat the like rela-
"tion of the daughter of a certaine noble
"and illustrious lord:" &c.

Bulwer's Philocophus, 112.

"I have been informed of an in-
"stance of a child who was come to be
"between eight and nine years of age,
"and had learned not only to *speak* but to
"read, when he *lost his hearing* by the
"small-pox, and continued deaf all his life
"after."

"VOX OCULIS SUBJECTA."

"after."—"At the age of *twenty-five* he was put under the care of a master, who professes *a most curious art*, of which I shall have occasion to make frequent mention, afterwards.—I mean the *teaching the deaf to speak*; this master * tells me, that, as he had been much neglected, after the loss of his hearing, (without the pains being bestowed upon him, that are commonly bestowed upon deaf persons) he found him, even at that advanced age, almost totally void of ideas, and was obliged to teach him to think, *as well as to speak*." Lord *Monboddo*'s Orig. and Prog. of Language, vol. I. p. 131.

The capacities for attaining *oral* or spoken language (besides the sense of hearing) are, *competent powers of mind, the voice*, and the common *organs of speech:*

* Mr. *Braidwood*.

now in healthy perfons ufually called dumb, there is no defect in either of thefe capacities, but the difficulty hath always been, to invent or create a fubftitute, for that fenfe * by which *others are enabled to imitate founds* (made fignificant by compact) or *words*. This difficulty hath been, until *lately*, (for fo I call the laft century,) deemed infuperable, but experience hath at laft evinced the contrary †.

Let

---

* Hearing.

† "We enter now upon the moft curious art of "*teaching* the *dumb* to *fpeak*, even when their deaf-"nefs continues. *This for many ages was thought im-*"*practicable, unlefs by means of a miracle.*—It is indeed "an undertaking of confiderable difficulty, and can "be accomplifhed only by time and degrees.—If fo "much time and attention be neceffary to attain the pro-"nunciation and knowledge of a foreign language, "even by thofe who enjoy the fenfe of hearing, how "much more muft it require in thofe who from their "infancy have been deprived of this benefit?—The "art of teaching the deaf and dumb to fpeak was "practifed about a century ago by Wallis, Holder,

"and

Let us take a summary view of those capacities just mentioned, in their order.

First, *the powers of the mind*, or soul—These are all comprized in the ability to perceive, and to will: and of *perception* and *volition* all language is only a representation. " Now the powers of the soul" (says the philosophical author of *Hermes*) " *over and above the mere nutritive*, may be
" included all of them in those of percep-
" tion and those of volition:— by the

" and others, but was carried to a superior degree by
" the learned and ingenious *Amman*.
   " This great anatomist, as *Boerhaáve* informs us,
" had inquired so minutely into the structure and ac-
" tion of the organs of speech, that, if his life had
" been longer preserved, he would have explained
" the physical causes of the various kinds of voice in
" other animals: he proceeded upon such simple and
" mechanical principles, that, provided his pupil was
" not of too dull an apprehension, *nor too far advan-*
" *ced* in years, nor had any material defect in his or-
" gans (of speech) *he would insure the success of his*
" *undertaking.*"   Herries' *Elem.* of speech.
                               " powers

" powers of perception, I mean, the *senses*
" *and the intellect*: by the powers of voli-
" tion, I mean in an extended sense, not
" only the will, but the several passions
" and appetites, *in short, all that moves* to
" action, whether rational or irrational."

The other senses of *seeing, feeling, tast-ing*, and *smelling*, enable men to perceive and distinguish space, solidity, figure, extention, motion, duration, succession, and colour, &c. as well as all *substances*, and their *qualities*, (altho' *they* know not their articulated forms or *names*, if naturally without hearing): it follows then, that, where *reason*, " that heaven-lighted lamp" is given, the power to *compare, compound, enlarge*, and *abstract* *, consequently the inclination to examine, measure, compute,

* Vide *Locke* on Understanding, respecting Ideas.

chuse

chuse or refuse, approve or disapprove, must be the necessary effect. Who will not allow, that naturally deaf persons are curiously inquisitive and observant; and as capable as any others of distinguishing *hardness* from *softness*, *motion* from *rest*, *unity* from *numbers,* *order* from *irregularity*, *beauty* from *deformity,* *smiles* from *frowns*, *grief* from *joy*, *sweetness* from *bitterness*, and in short *(excepting those of sounds)* all *painful* sensations from *pleasureable?*—Who will deny, when they invariably, from the dictates of their own minds, or from the example and representation of others, avoid or decline whatever is or may be *hurtful*, *disgustful,* or *ugly* and *unpleasing;* and cheafully seek, embrace, and prefer what hath a rational probability of being *innocent, agreable,* and *eligible,* that they manifest (as clearly as hearing men) the powers of *perception* (both by sensation and

and reflexion) and of *volition*; which comprehend all the leading powers of the soul*?

The generality of the world are apt suddenly, but mistakenly, to combine the idea of ideotism with that of the state of the deaf and dumb, whereas no greater error can subsist, as may plainly appear by the instances of perfection to which many (who have been taught by *Mess. Braidwoods*) have arrived in language, and other arts, as well as in the sciences:—the truth is, that the scale of intellectual comprehensions, or understandings, in them, is as *variously graduated* as in other persons; many of them, indeed, possess a quickness of apprehension, a scope of *imagination*,

---

* " Since *Pain* and pleasure seem to be as much
" the *Origin* of the different forms of worship, *as*
" *they are of the ideas of mankind.*"
Abbé Raynal, Hist. of Ind.
and

and sagacity, *above* the common standard among those who are *not* naturally deaf: in proof of which, some specimens of their compositions will be found in the affixed appendix, the genuine production of such persons now living.

The voice is the next requisite; the source and fountain of this are the *lungs*, which, it is well known, are the primary efficient cause of respiration or breathing;—voice is only breath made sonorous in its passage through the wind-pipe, by the contraction of that interior part of the *larynx*, called the *glottis*, which is a small chink, of a gristly, tremulous substance, peculiarly fitted for the production of sound, by the vibration of air, upon its sides, and thro' its orifice, which are capable of such extention and contraction, firmness or relaxation, as may be necessary for effecting the different vocal sounds.

" Hence

"Hence it is," (says *Herries*) "that the *glottis* bears a near resemblance to both a *wind* and a *stringed instrument*, the one from its form, the other from its substance."—All sound arises from an impulse communicated by some tremulous body to the particles of air.—This vibration, which always accompanies a vocal tone, is clearly *perceptible to the sight and touch:* it is evident, that the tone in the human throat arises from similar causes to that in an instrument. When we blow into the orifice of *a flute,* the stream of air expelled through so narrow a chink becomes forceable and rapid, dashes against the particles in the body of the instrument, and by dislodging them produces the sound. The same effect is occasioned by expelling the breath through the *contracted* glottis. When we strike the strings of a *violin,*

"they

"they vibrate and refound, in the fame manner, the fmooth griftly chords of the *glottis* are excited into a tremulous motion in the production of found."

None of thefe parts on which the voice depends, have neceffarily any immediate connexion with the organs of hearing, confequently they may be perfect, while thofe are imperfect; and dumb men may have as good voices, naturally, as any other perfons: the fact is, that they not only have, but, that they ufe them alfo; although very *uncouthly*, and without articulation, (*until inftructed*). Such children, alfo, cry, and laugh, exactly as all other children do.

The organs of fpeech are the only remaining neceffary qualification.

It is by the various positions and actions of these, that articulation is effected: therefore, they are *all* essentially requisite in oral language; every impulse of voice receiving its particular modification, or alteration, from those different positions.

They are too well known to need description;—every one, having these organs in proper proportion, viz. *tongue*, *lips*, lower *jaw*, *teeth*, *gums*, palate, *uvula*, and *nostrils*, is capable of effecting all the configurations that produce the elementary sounds; which any one may very easily convince himself of, only by running over (with the voice) the alphabet, and observing the different action of these organs respectively.

A complete set of these instruments, in perfect symmetry, are *generally* found to
be

"VOX OCULIS SUBJECTA."

be possessed by the dumb:—for their want of speech, as hath been before asserted, doth not proceed from any impediment herein, but merely from want of hearing.

And here, it is impossible, in reflecting upon the *infinite wisdom* and *contrivance* manifested in the construction of these organs of speech, and those of hearing, *not to be struck with astonishment*, and realize that

" The hand that made us is *divine* *."

So " *fearfully* and *wonderfully* are we made."

Having now, as proposed, cursorily considered *the powers of the mind, the voice,* and *the organs of speech*, and observed

* " For farther investigating how much better the
" parts of the organs of speech are framed for dif-
" course in man, (*who is a discursive* animal) than in
" in other animals, vide *Aristot. Treatise de Anima.*
" *Par.* lib. II. c. 17.—lib. III. c. 1; 3. *de Anima*, lib.
" II. c. 8." Harris's Hermes.

that, the predicament in which the dumb (in general) are, doth not refult from any deficiency in either of *thofe capacites*, it may clearly be inferred, that (where that is the cafe) if any fubftitute for the fenfe of hearing can be adopted, *the faculty or art of communication by fpeech may be acquired by them*, altho' with greater application and difficulty, and longer perfeverance, than by thofe who (their ears being perfect) are enabled to regulate and modulate their voices, by imitation, according to their perception of founds.

It is by the refpective nerves of each fenfe, that the feveral perceptions of all their objects are conducted to the brain: *hearing* by the *auditory* nerve, *feeing* by the *optic*, tafting by thofe of the tongue and palate, *fmelling* by the *olfactory*, and *feeling* by the genus nervofum, or nervous fyftem, system, which pervades and overspreads the whole structure of the body. If by the optic nerve, a perception can be conveyed to the brain, which shall virtually excite the same idea in the soul, as that excited by the conveyance of the auditory nerve, the first and principal step is gained; which is to understand the meaning of a word or words, *by the form*, instead *of the sound*.—The signification of words in general is merely arbitrary, there being no analogy or natural resemblance of the sounds to the thing signified, for instance, *horse, man, ball, bat, cow, &c.*—It is by *repeating the sounds*, and pointing out the object, to children universally, that they come by degrees to understand what those sounds signify.—By the same method (*mutatis mutandis*) changing *sounds* for *forms*, may children without hearing, be taught to know the *names* and *qualities* of every thing animate and inanimate, and underſtand them when uttered or written, which is the foundation of all language whatever. It is true, that the forms of words, even in writing or print, are not likeneſſes of the things they are made to repreſent, any more than ſounds are, but they are as much ſo; and are found more completely convenient for the purpoſes of language, than abſolute pictures, or hieroglyphics; but this relates only to *written, not oral* language.—Words, however, have a *form* in utterance, as well as in characters, and this form is, by habit, diſcernible by the eye*.—Of ſome words, much more ſo, un-

---

* " *Fabricius* makes all this good, by a familiar
" and eaſie example: for when he was a ſchooleboy,
" there being many of them in one chamber, they
" were interdicted the uſe of ſpeech. But we"
(ſaith he) " by the *motion* only of our *lips and tongue*,
" without any voyce at all, altho' we were diſtant one
" from another, did communicate our conceptions,
" and

undoubtedly, than others; *for example*
how easily may the form of the word *paw*

"and affections of mind one unto another: and a
"curiosity of constant observation hath enabled many
"to doe as much: for *Ludovicus Vives* speaks of some
"artists, who could discover what any man spake;
"tho' no sound of their intent approached their eare
"descrying the stillest and low voyced words of their
"lips, helped by an art-informing and *attentive eye*,
"*onely by seeing their lips to move and open as they do in*
"*speech*. It is likewise related of ancient Dr. *Gabriel*
"*Neale*, that he could understand any word by the
"mere *motion* of the *lips* without any *audible utterance*.
"And Sir *William Cornwallys*, speaking of a lover,
"attributes such a faculty to him: his eares (saith
"he) not having ability to perform their office, he
"therefore teacheth his eyes a *new occupation*, mea-
"suring the wind that proceedeth from his mistresses
"mouth, and spelling *words* by the observation of
"her *lips*. But we cannot wish for a more ample tes-
"timony of this thing than the usual practice of those
"friends of Mr. *Crispes*, who being intimate with him,
"in their familiar conversation never used their voyce,
"but saved themselves the unnecessary labor of speak-
"ing out, exhibiting only the motions of speech dis-
"tinctly to him, without any other sound than that
"of their pure motion, which is audible enough to
"him who *wore his eare in his eye*: sound and the
"voyce adding nothing of perfection to the intelli-
"gible *motions* of articulate speech."

Bulwer's Philoc. p. 52.

be perceived; that is the position and action of the organs in forming it.—It is the effect of only *compressing the lips very closely*, then letting *fall the lower jaw and lip*, and *at the same time breathing*, strongly, (so strongly as to make the vocal sound*).

Thus far respects only the means of knowing what may be uttered by others without hearing them, but how shall a *deaf person* himself pronounce, or *express* those sounds, which he hath never heard? — Here the assistance of another sense besides that of sight offers itself, and is greatly conducive to this happy effect. I

---

* " It would be a good way of teaching children
" *(in general)* to speak soon plain, by shewing them
" the *motions* of the mouth and tongue, for the pro-
" nouncing each letter and syllable; and by this way,
" *people from their nativity deaf,* have learned to speak,
" and by knowing, *the motions for such words, to*
" *know when they were uttered.*"
Beare's *Sensorium*, p. 108, printed in 1710.

mean

mean *feeling*, which is said to be the universal sense, *the most necessary*, and to which all the others (indeed) may be reduced, because by the *tact* the impression of all objects are made on their respective organs *—Of the use of *feeling* in *this case* some farther description shall be given in the course of this *attempt*.

Wherever nature has denied or withheld one of the five senses, she has kindly compensated by an *uncommon* degree of perfection in the others.—The extraordinary vigilance of those senses in possession, is very obvious in all such instances.—Thus the blind are good *musicians* † and *mathematicians* ‡, and as such are capable of

---

* Vide Campanella de Sensu Rerum.

† Mr. *Stanley*—The Rev. Dr. *Blacklock* of Edinburgh, blind from his infancy, and others.

‡ Dr. *Sanderson*, formerly Lucasian Professor of Mathematics at Cambridge, born blind.

forming juſt ideas (by ſound and *touch*) of the motion, figure, ſize, and diſtance of objects, their numbers, and relative proportions.

Now may it not eaſily be credited, that ſuch *blind* perſons have a perfect notion of many machines; ſuch as wheel-carriages, by feeling and handling the different parts? Can they not alſo determine, by the ſounds they make (when paſſing over a hard ſurface) not only the *diſtance*, but the *courſe*, and *velocity* of ſuch paſſing carriages, altho' this be the proper province of viſion?—This faculty, however, *it muſt be noticed*, is the reſult of habit and repeated obſervation.

As thus we find the ſenſe of *hearing*, aided by the touch, or ſenſe of feeling, can in *ſome inſtances* do the duty of the eye, ſo we ſhall be convinced that the ſenſe of
ſeeing

seeing (with the same assistance) can do as much for the ear *.

From the supposed universality of speech, and the seeming facility with which it is gradually acquired in childhood, even by the most ignorant and uninstructed in society, we are apt to consider language as born with us, like the senses, or rather not to consider it at all.—The organs of speech are as necessary for *chusing, preparing,* and *conducting* animal sustenance to the stomach, as for articulation, and *those* are the first and indeed only *natural* uses of them (strictly speaking): the latter is artificial. —By *articulation* I do *not* mean the utterance or production of the mere *vocal sounds*; but the expression of syllables, or words, composed of consonants and vowels.

* Vide *Lord Bacon*'s Natural History, respecting the consent of *audibles* and *visibles*.

Speech is with every individual of the human race a gradual acquisition; we are *all, mute,* at first, or when nature pushes us upon this theatre of life, altho' endowed with *capacities,* and dispositions, for learning this and other arts.—At our birth, and for a long time after, have we any more language, than any irrational animal? Are we not, as we come from the hands of nature, a " *mutum pecus*" (a mute herd) as Horace truely calls us? — As no man (whatever might be his genius) was ever an artist at once, or complete master of any art or faculty by intuition, or nature, (that is without instruction, or *imitation of others,* who had by a long succession of experiments and practice, begun and completed the system;) so, neither was ever a child born with the faculty of speech, notwithstanding some absurd, ridiculous legends of *superstitious* or designing priests and others

" VOX OCULIS SUJBECTA."

to that purpofe *. Articulation, or founds formed into words of meaning, is therefore certainly not † natural to mankind, but

* " An infant is called *infans, quafi non fans*, so that is remarkable, which *Hali Abben Ragel* reports, that he faw an infant who beganne to fpeake when he was fcarce *twenty-four houres old*, since he was borne unhappily to foretell the loffe of the kingdom, and the deftruction and defolation of that nation."

" Anno 633, *Nanthildis*, the wife of king *Dagobert* the fecond, brought him a fon which was named *Sigibertus*: this infant being forty days old, when he was to be chriften'd by *St. Amandus* the bifhop, when they were all filent, he *anfwered* with a clear voice *Amen*."

" Anno 1275, in *Cracovia* a certaine infant *fcarce halfe a yeare old*, beganne *diftinctly* and *readily* to fpeake, and fay, to the great admiration of all, *The Tartars fhall come, and cut off our heads*, and when he was afked whether he was not afraid himfelfe of the *Tartars*, he anfwered, *Yea, in good footh, I am in great dread of them, becaufe they fhall take away my head alfo*, which came to pafs twelve years after."

Bulwer's Philoc. *publifhed* 1648, p. 5 and 6.

Rifum teneatis amici!

† " The gift of fpeech is not the gift of nature to man, but like many others acquired by him."— For a more full proof of this affertion, vid. Lord *Monboddo's* Orig. and Prog. of Lang. vol. I. pp. 12—177.

intirely the effect of art; this art hath been from rude beginnings brought to its present degree of perfection, in a succeffion of ages, in proportion to the multiplication of arts, and always keeping pace with the progrefs of refinements, in society.

There is no such thing as an univerfal language, unlefs we allow *inarticulate* cries (or founds) and geftures (or figns) to be language: and in that fenfe, the brutes may be faid to have a language as well as mankind.——If articulate language were natural to man, muft it not follow that the fame would be *common* to every nation, and fpoken *fpontaneoufly* by all of the fame fpecies (having the organs of pronunciation); and of courfe, that perfons born *deaf* would have it as perfectly as any? for they have all *faculties* that others *enjoy from nature,* and what in that case should hinder their possession of this?

It is intellect, or abilities of reasoning and imitation, with the powers of imagination, which form the exalted and distinguishing prerogative of human nature, and these, as was before observed, are not wanting in persons born *deaf*, although language always is; (that is without *peculiar* instruction:)—a capacity also of acquiring every faculty or art, except music, and oratory; (which is a species of music) with all the necessary *means* of pronunciation, nature hath absolutely (although under great disadvantages indeed) bestowed on them; but, by want of the perception of sounds, they are exactly in the same state, with respect to speech, which we may suppose any persons would be in, who were shut up, and bred together, from earliest infancy, in a place and manner which should render it impossible for them to hear any language spoken;—that is, *without speech*.

Sir *Kenelm Digby*, in his Treatise of Bodies, mentions a remarkable instance of one John of Liege, who, from the apprehensions of danger from an approaching enemy, took shelter in a forest, and was lost, where he remained so long that he quite lost the use of speech, and had it to learn again; whereas had language been natural, and not acquired, he *could not* have *lost* it.

Here, perhaps, a plausible objection will be started,—

" Was Adam speechless? Had he any
" example, by the imitation of which he ac-
" quired language, to enable him to give
" names

"names to every living creature, or to an-
"swer the Voice of the Lord in the gar-
"den of Eden? and if Adam had this
"faculty, by nature, why not his heirs
"and succeffors when they arrive at the
"ftate of maturity?"

To this it is replied, that many *learned* and *pious* divines have agreed, that the metaphorical ftyle fo much in ufe in the eaft, and with which the Holy Scriptures of the Old Teftament abound, may account for this: they have accordingly been of opinion, that it is *figurative* expreffion, not ftrictly hiftorical, in the fame manner, as, in the fame chapter, the *Immaterial, Omnifcient Spirit*, or Firft Caufe, is faid to have *brought* every living creature unto *Adam*, to *see* * what he would *call* them; and as the

---

* " And out of the ground the *Lord God* formed
" *every beaft* of the field, and *every fowl* of the air,
" and

the *serpent's* * *language* to Eve, together with many other similar instances, more especially the following, " And it *repented* the " Lord that he had made man, on the " earth; and it *grieved him at the heart* †," " which they think, *strictly* speaking, (and so do I) *cannot be possible.*—Allowing, however, the former, respecting Adam's giving names to the animals, to be strictly historical, the objection is removeable, in another way; for we may well suppose, and believe, that the Infinite Wisdom and Goodness might, by a miraculous exertion of the same Almighty Power, which gave the first man existence, also qualify him for the state he was in, by imparting to him,

---

" and *brought* them unto Adam, *to see* what he would
" call them, and whatever Adam *called* every living
" creature, *that* was the name thereof."
       Gen. chap. ii. ver. 19.
 * " And the serpent *said* unto the woman, Ye shall
" not surely die."   Gen. ch. iii. ver. 4.
 † Gen. ch. vi. ver. 6.

intuitively, such a degree of language as was necessary to his *unprecedented*, artless * and innocent condition; as the apostles were instantaneously inspired, *for a particular occasion*, with the gift of † "Tongues", (or languages); but that necessity ceasing, with respect to his posterity, *the miraculous gift of speech*, without example, might cease also, as it certainly did to the immediate descendants of the Apostles.

But, be these reasonings just or erroneous, whatever might have been Adam's faculties,

---

* " Pride then was not, nor *arts* that pride to aid,
" Man walk'd with beast, *joint tenant* of the shade.
" Essay on *Man*."

† " And they were filled with the Holy Ghost, and
" *began to speak* with *other tongues*, as the spirit gave
" them utterance." Acts ch. ii. ver. 4.

" Parthians and Medes and Elamites, the dwellers
" in Mesopotamia, and in Judea, and Cappadocia, in
" Pontus and Asia,—Phrygia and Pamphilia in Egypt,
" and in the parts of Libya, about Cyrene, and
" strangers

faculties, *we know*, that his offspring do *not* inherit any such, not only for the reasons already given, respecting infants, (who, let them be born of what parents they may, learn *only* the language of the people with whom they are brought up) but, because all the wild men that have been found without society, have been found also *without speech*, of which there are sundry instances *; and because *we know* also, that many savage tribes, who are not absolutely

---

" strangers of Rome, Jews and proselytes,—Cretes,
" and Arabians, do we hear them speak *in our tongues*,
" the wonderful works of God." Ibid. ver. 9, 10, 11.

* Several solitary savages have been found in *Europe*, at different times, *all mute*, or without articulation, which, however, some of them *soon* acquired, by imitation, viz.

1st, One near Hesse Cassell, in 1344, *mute* when taken, but *taught to speak*.

Vide Rousseau sur *l'Inegalité* des Hommes.
2d, Another in the Forest of Lithuania in 1694.
3d, Others in the Pyrenian Mountains, 1719— and the Hanoverian in the reign of *Geo.* I. &c.

Monboddo's Orig. and Prog. of Lang.

without

without society (although possessed of very few arts,) have at this day, such an *imperfect* system as plainly proves it a progressive acquisition*, therefore it matters not whether Adam had a particular language of articulation, or not, *ab initio*; it being evident, that the human race have not uniformly and inevitably received *this legacy* from him †. Having, it is hoped, obviated this scruple, let us proceed,

" Say

---

* The *Huron* tribe, and others.

† " If therefore the human voice is only the imi-
" tation of such sounds as are most familiar to us, or
" in which we are most carefully instructed, it must
" follow that the *ear* is the medium by which these
" sounds are conveyed. *What then must be the situa-*
" *tion of those who from their infancy* have been *deprived*
" *of hearing?*—They must *naturally* be speechless.—
" They always are.—If it was *natural* for man to speak,
" he would exert that action as soon as the organs were
" capable, *whether he was taught* or not.—But if no such
" instance can be found, where a person *born deaf* was
" ever known to utter articulate speech (*unless from the*
" *mechanical*

> "Say firſt, of GOD above, or *man below*,
> "What can we reaſon, but from what *we*
> "*know?*"   POPE.

How manifeſt a truth is it, "that man differs more from man, than man from beaſt?" becauſe by that cultivation of his *capacities*, which is called education, he is, in a manner, metamorphoſed, into almoſt another, and, ſuperior ſpecies!

It is ſuppoſed, by the Author of the Origin and Progreſs of Language (a very learned, *curious*, and philoſophical work), and the ſuppoſition ſupported with great ingenuity and probability, that *mankind* have been gradually emerging from a ſtate

---

"*mechanical principles in the laſt ſection)* we may then
"ſafely conclude, that the *art of ſpeaking*, is as much
"the effect of *imitation* and *ſkill*, as the *art* of *writing*,
"or of *playing* upon *the harpſichord.*"
  Herries' Elem. of Speech, p. 88.

of barbarism; that they have, from being originally, wild, savage creatures, been tamed, and humanized; and improved by cultivation, and the introduction of the various arts found by experience necessary to society; but, that society *may* have existed for *ages, before* a system of articulate *language was invented.*—In this there is certainly no impossibility, as he says, inasmuch as persons remaining absolutely *dumb* are known to be *capable of living together in society, of communicating,* in some degree, *the knowledge of their wants, of carrying on conjointly any sort of business, and of governing and directing:*—he adduces also in proof, that even some of the brutes are capable of the same; viz. the beaver, and *ourang outang,* which latter (by the way) *he fancies* to be of the human species, and quotes *Rousseau* to confirm it.

It,

It, however, doth not appear to me romantic, to suppose, with him, that, at first, *in a state of nature*, the substitutes for language were murmuring inarticulate sounds; that barbarous nations could only express their different passions by different cries, similar to the instances we are acquainted with in the *war-hoop*, the *cry of success*, and others, in practice among the American Indians;—that articulation, or the dividing, by consonants, the continuity of the vocal sounds, was, *at first*, very simple;—it still continues very much so among the Huron tribe, an *interior* nation of North America: their language is the least removed, (as he says very justly) from the origin of this art, of perhaps any upon earth*: — " They have scarcely " even any articulation, but converse chief-

---

* Gab. Sagard and La Hontane give this account of them.

" ly

"ly by vocal cries afpirated, as in falutation, for example, *ho, ho, ho,* ufing very few confonants, and of courfe in fpeaking never clofe their lips: in fhort, their language is little better than animal cries from the throat, of different tones, divided now and then by a guttural confonant: and without compofition or derivation."—This is alfo nearly the cafe with feveral other barbarous people:— The vowels, which are the firft of the elemental founds, are always uttered with little or no action of the mouth, being nothing elfe but breath vocalized, by the vibration of the interior parts of the throat, and paffing through the organs of the mouth in certain peculiar pofitions; thus *A* is only breath blown hard, with an open mouth; *O* is founded in like manner, only by forming the lips into a circle: —the other vowels, with little variation, are

are upon the same easy principle.—The junction of consonants to these vowels, by a further modification of the several positions and actions of the tongue, teeth, palate, and lips (assisted by the nose and throat more or less) forms those alterations of the voice, or division of the continuity of vocal sounds, which is properly, *articulation:* without this speech would only be a cluster of vocal cries, with little distinction.

The vowels being the foundation of speech, and uttered with so little art, or action of the mouth, is doubtless the reason, that among savages, language (if it deserves to be so called) chiefly consists of vowels, for they have not advanced the art to any great degree: they use words like young children who are beginning to speak, without any connectives: they have no syntax,

syntax, but in lieu thereof, a vaſt variety of tones and abundance of action.—This perhaps hath been, at one time or another, the ſtate of language in all thoſe nations or tribes of mankind, from which the preſent proud nations of the earth have proceeded. — That theſe uncultivated tribes, and all others, are the offspring of Adam, thoſe who make the beforementioned obection muſt conſequently allow.

The hiſtory of man in various ages and countries, and the nature of things, ſufficiently prove, that the *only natural* language of our ſpecies is a variety of *vocal* ſounds and tones, ſignificant of our wants or deſires, accompanied by ſigns with the head, hand, &c. and the management of the countenance, ſo as (imperfectly) to expreſs the diſpoſition of mind, and the will.—In proceſs of time, thoſe muttering noiſes have been

art.-

articulated *, to such a number as the sensible objects then existing required *names* for, which names were (it is probable) simply descriptive, at first, of their most striking qualities, or appearances: as children are observed to distinguish animals by their different *noises, roarings,* or *bleatings,* before they know the arbitrary appellations of such animals: For instance, *Bow, Wow,* (for dog) *Bah* (lamb) *Moo* (cow) and such like.—Thus language grew by degrees, on which alterations were grafted, and in proportion to the necessity, variety of words ensued, until by an infinite multiplication of such articulated sounds, method be-

---

* " I say *articulation*, because there *may be other* " ways of discriminating the voice, e. g.—by *acuteness* " and *gravity,* the several degrees of rising and fall- " ing from one note or *tone* to another, and the se- " veral kinds of measures, passions, moods, ayre, &c. " out of which it were easie to frame *a language, with-* " *out words*, tho' not so expedite and comprehensive " as the other."   *Holder's* Elem. of Speech, p. 18.

came

came indispensibly necessary to avoid confusion, to denote *qualities, action, time, quantity, connexion,* and (by " *substance,* " *energy,* and *subject*") to convey ideas intelligibly *.

The method used in teaching those who are by nature without hearing to speak,

* In the same manner, therefore, as *local motion* is from nature, but *dancing* is something *positive*; so is the *power* of producing a *vocal sound* founded *in nature*, but that of explaining ourselves by nouns and verbs, *something positive*: and hence it is, that, as to the *simple power* of producing *vocal* sound (*which* is as it were the instrument of the soul's faculties of knowledge and volition), as to this vocal power, I say, man *seems* to possess it from nature *in the like manner as irrational animals*, but as to the employing nouns or verbs †, or sentences composed out of them, in the explanation of our sentiments (*the things thus employed* being founded *not* in nature, but in *position*) *this*, he seems to possess by way of peculiar eminence, *because* he alone of all mortal beings, *partakes* of a *soul* which can move of itself, &c.

Ammonius de Interpretatione, p. 51.

† Some of the ancients divided the whole of language, as a system, into *nouns* and *verbs*.

and

and the progress observable in them, may serve in some measure to confirm this :— they at first use cries, only, or uncouth irregular exertions of voice, with signs, until art, in other words precept, and example, regulate these sounds :—the first advance is made by an ingenious method of sounding the vowels, (of which some further explanation will be given in the sequel) as the notes of the gamut are commonly at first learned, without any connection with time, or that arrangement which is called a tune: when the five vowels can be distinctly sounded and discriminated, then an easy monosyllable is learned, as *Ba, Be,* &c. ; for, besides the distinct sound of the vowel, it is only *the compression of the lips,* before utterance of the vowel, that makes the syllable, *Ba,* and so on.—Having acquired syllables, (of the combination of which the longest world or *polysyllable* is made) all words of course may be pronounced:—*for example*, taking first a *word* of one syllable.—Suppose the learner to be perfect in pronouncing *Ba*; then by placing the tongue in such a position as to add *T*, (which is no more than pressing the top of the tongue close against the upper gum) the word *Bat* is formed: thus articulation of one word is learned, in which two out of three letters are consonants.—Being perfect in the pronunciation, he next attains *the idea*, which *this form of articulated breath* conveys, by having the object or thing itself placed before his eyes, and pointed at; thus he knows the name of *Bat*, and when he sees it again, or when the idea of the thing so called occurs to his mind, he knows how to utter its name.—He soon easily learns to distinguish persons, as *Charles, William, John,* by the prepositive pronouns singular,

F   I,

I, You, He; alfo the words fignifying the moft common and familiar actions, as *eat, drink, walk*; next the connexion of fubftantive and attributive, or noun and verb, as *I (Charles) eat, you (William) drink, he (John) walks*, then (fuppofing him firft to have learned the *form* (in writing and fpeech) and the meaning of *bread*) he compofes a compleat fentence, as *I eat bread*, and afterwards fentences lefs fimple. — This is the natural progrefs of the art of fpeech, and whoever will take the pains to attend to the gradual advances therein made, by children, in general, cannot fail to obferve it.—The chief difference is, that fuch as hear, make a variety of experiments with their organs of fpeech, to imitate the founds they hear, before they hit upon the right pofition to effect it; but, at length, by perfeverance, and repeatedly comparing by their ear their own

pro

production of sounds with that of others, they arrive at just articulation; *generally*, however, long before they know the nature of many things whose names they pronounce: beginning usually with those easy words in which the consonants are labials, or formed wholly by the lips, as *Pa pa*, *Ma ma* *, &c.—whereas those, who are void of hearing, learn *(or are taught)* to vocalize and articulate their breath, by *feeling* and *seeing*, instead of by the other sense, and arrive at the knowledge of the connexion and import of words and sentences, by inculcation and study of their *forms*, in characters, and in enunciation in lieu of the more easy mode, which hearing persons enjoy.—The

---

* " That this is the natural order, and that the lips
" are the first organs of speech, exerted by children,
" may be known from this, that the words *Papa*, or
" *Baba*, and *Mama*, are the terms, used by children
" for Father and Mother, in almost all the languages
" of the world." Sheridan's Art of Reading, p. 39.

former may be compared to perfons who acquire the *art* of mufic by rote, or merely by their own *imitative* powers and *endeavours*, the latter to thofe who are *taught it* by inftructors, fyftematically.

What is the inference from the preceding propofitions?

The inference intended is, that the only natural language, already defcribed, may be methodized and formed into a practicable, intelligible fyftem, *by all poffeffed of underftanding*, of the *inftruments* of *voice*, and *articulation*.

Taking for granted that it will be allowed, with refpect to thofe who are bleffed with the ufual important fenfe of hearing; it remains only to be proved, that it is practicable and intelligible likewife by the *deaf*.

Is

Is it incredible that, a perfon void of hearing, may by *feeling* the vibration, or efficient caufe of *vocal* founds in the throat, *inwardly*, and by application of the touch *outwardly*, in contradiftinction to the *mere* impulfes of breath, learn by perfeverance and affiftance, to know when he gives the different tremulous motions of the air, which we diftinguifh by the vocal founds, *A, E, I, O, U?*

Is it incredible, that fuch a perfon afterwards by attentively looking at others when fpeaking, and by *feeing* how they place their *lips* and tranpofe their *tongue*, occafionally, to the *teeth, gums,* and *palate*, for the combination of the confonants and vowels, fhould learn in time, to imitate the pronunciation of all the various fyllables, which immediately compofe words, and eventually language?

All words are modified undulations of air, made fignificant to the mind, by focial compact, or confent.—The firft ftep to language is to *form them*, the next to *comprehend* their meaning.—It hath been already premifed that vowels are the fundamentals, and expreffed with little or no action of the loquelary organs, like feparate, fimple notes in a flute, independent of *time*, flats, fharps, refts, &c.—That when thefe are learned by the method juft hin ed at, articulation of the moft eafy fyllables is next to be inculcated, fhewing the *form, in writing*, as well as in utterance, at the fame time;—thus bringing the pupil gradually on from fyllables to words, from words to fentences, firft fimple, then compound, until he becomes capable of every kind of compofition.

It may well be fuppofed, that *the method* of inftructing fuch deaf perfons muft be

ex-

extremely tedious, and laborious *to the teacher*, and the greatest possible trial of his patience; but it is the purpose of this essay to prove, that it *hath been* reduced to practice, and that *it is* practised with great success, *at present*, rather than to attempt to describe *particularly* the ingenious mode in use. If a person can be brought to speak at all, and is not deficient in intellects, application and perseverance in a judicious method may enable him, *most undoubtedly*, to make vast improvements in the faculty of speech: this is demonstrated in the removal of the most violent impediments of stammerers, which is also completely effected by the same gentlemen who profess the other art, of which more in its place:—the greatest orator of Greece was at first almost an unintelligible stutterer: by long labour and indefatigable perseverance, he overcame all difficulties, and in spite of nature became the paragon of eloquence: his soliloquizing on the sea-coast near the roaring surges, with pebbles in his mouth (if true) strongly supports the argument that the use of articulate language is not only, *not natural*, but slowly progressive and of difficult acquisition, although it may be attained, by right application and long practice, even under the greatest disadvantages.—" *labor omnia vincit.*"

It is not, however, pretended that *Demosthenes* is any instance in proof that the *deaf* may acquire speech;—but so true is it that the *voice is governable by the eyes,* that the gentlemen, to whose merits this art is indebted for its present degree of perfection, have *publicly* adopted as their *motto*, the phrase which is borrowed for the title of these pages, viz.

" vox

"VOX OCULIS SUBJECTA,"
or (as it *may* be englifhed)
Voice made vifible.

After all that has been advanced, conviction may be ftill wanting to many:— *Facts*, however, are incontrovertible, and witneffes or vouchers of *facts in point*, are at hand, " out of the mouths and pens of *more than* two credible witneffes the fact fhall be eftablifhed".

The following paffages are extracted from the feveral beforementioned, in order of time, who have treated on this fubject, and borne teftimony to the various fuccefs of the art in *fome few inftances*; after which the author's own evidence fhall be given.

Firft—

First—Extract* from Dr. *Bulwer's* Philocophus, or *Deaf* and Dumb Man's Friend, printed 1648.

"CHAP. XV.

"So lazie and fluggifh are the naturall
"inclinations of moſt men, that they are
"prone to limit the infinite capacity of
"man, and the effects of his admirable
"obſervations to known and common
"matters: whereas, confidering his abili-
"ties, and the faculty of his braine, there
"is no accident of imperfection that may
"befall him, but with the indulgent co-
"operation of nature, he may worke
"himſelfe either out of it, or invent a
"ſupply to the defect and inconveniences
"of it: for a notable inſtance of the in-
"duſtrious felicity of an obſerving wit in
"this kind, wee are extraordinarily be-
"holden to that gallant and learned knight

* N.B. The *ſpelling* in theſe extracts is copied exactly from the *original.*

" *Sir*

"*Sir Kenelme Digby.* That whereas hitherto the underſtanding of *words* by the *motions of the lips* hath been an art which we have heard indeed that many have pretended thereunto, yet hath it been thought *deccitful* and ſcarce to be credited, he affords us an example of an artiſt, who ſublimed this art unto an *almoſt* incredible perfection.

"The hiſtory of this rare atchievement of art is thus delivered by *that honourable relator* Sir Kenelme Digby.

"There was a nobleman of great quality that I knew in *Spaine,* the younger brother of the Conſtable of *Caſtile,* who was taught to *heare* the *ſounds of words* with his *eyes* (if this expreſſion may be permitted). This Spaniſh lord was born *deafe,* ſo deafe that if a gun were ſhott off cloſe by his *eare* he could not heare it, and conſequently

"quently he was *dumbe*; for not being
"able to heare the sound of words, he
"could never imitate nor understand them:
"the lovelinesse of his face, and especially
"the exceeding life and spiritfulnesse of
"his eyes, and the comlinesse of his
"person, and the whole composure of his
"body throughout, were pregnant signes
"of a well temper'd mind within, and
"therefore all that knew him lamented
"much the want of meanes to cultivate it,
"and to embrue it with the notions which
"it seem'd to be capable of, in regard of
"itselfe, had it not been crofs'd by this
"unhappy accident, which to remedy phy-
"sitions and chyrurgions had long em-
"ploy'd their skill, but all in vaine. At
"the last there was a priest who under-
"tooke the teaching him to understand
"others when they spoke, and to *speake*
"himselfe that others might understand
"him,

"him, for which attempt at first he was
"laugh'd at, yet *after some years* he was
"look'd upon as if he had wrought a
"miracle. In a word, after *strange pa-*
"*tience, constancie,* and *pains,* he brought
"the young lord to speak as distinctly as
"any man whatsoever; and to understand
"so perfectly what they said, that he
"would not loose a word in a whole dayes
"conversation. I have often discoursed
"with the priest, whilst I waited upon
"the prince of Wales (now our gracious
"sovereign) in Spaine, and I doubt not
"but his majesty remembreth all I have
"said of him, and much more: for *his*
"*majesty was very curious to observe,* and
"enquire into it. It is true, one great
"misbecomingnesse he was apt to fall into
"whilst he spoke: which was an uncer-
"tainty in the tone of his voice, for not
"hearing the sound he made when he
"spoke,

"spoke, he could not steadily govern the
"pitch of his voice, but it would be some-
"times higher and sometimes lower, though
"for the most part what he delivered toge-
"ther, he ended in the same key as he
"began it. But when he had once suf-
"fered the passage of his voice to close,
"at the opening it again, chance, or the
"measure of his earnestnesse to speake or
"reply, gave him his tone, which he was not
"capable of modulating by such an artifice
"as is recorded Caius Gracchus used when
"passion in his orations to the people
"drove out his voice with too great a ve-
"hemence or shrillnesse. He could dis-
"cern in another whether he spoke shrill
"or low, and he would repeat after any
"body any hard word whatsoever, which
"the prince tried often, not only in *Eng-
"lish*, but by making some *Welch* men that
"served his highnesse speake words of
"their language, which he so perfectly
"ecchoed,

" ecchoed, that I confesse I wondred more
" at that, than at all the rest; and his
" master himselfe would acknowledge that
" the rules of his art reached not to
" produce that effect with any certainty.
" And therefore concluded this in him
" must spring from other rules he had
" framed unto himselfe out of his own at-
" tentive observation; which the advantage
" which nature had justly given him in
" the sharpnesse of senses, to supply the
" want of this, endowed him with an abi-
" lity and sagacity, to do *beyond* any other
" man that had his hearing. He expressed
" it surely in a high measure by his so
" exact imitation of the *Welch* pronuncia-
" tion: for that tongue (like the *Hebrew*)
" employeth much the guttural letters, and
" the motions of that part which frameth
" them, cannot be seen or judged of by
" the eye, otherwise than by the effect

" they

"they may happily make by confent in
"the other parts of the mouth expofed to
"view. For the knowledge he had of
"what they faid fprung from his obferving
"the motions they made, fo that he could
"converfe currently in the light, though
"they he talked to, whifpered never fo
"foftly. And I have feen him at a dif-
"tance of a large chamber's breadth, *fay*
"*words* after one, that I, ftanding clofe
"by the fpeaker, could not hear a fylla-
"ble of. But, if he were in the darke,
"or if one turned his face out of his
"fight, he was capable of nothing one
"faid." Sir Kenelme Digby.

Secondly—Extract from Dr. *Holder*.

"March 4, 166⅔.
"At a meeting of the Council of the Royal
"Society, ordered,
"That a Difcourfe prefented to the R.
"Society, intituled Elements of Speech,

" or an Essay of Enquiry into the Natural
" Production of Letters, with an Appendix
" concerning Persons *Deaf* and *Dumb* by
" *W. Holder, D. D. Fellow of the Royal So-*
" *ciety, be printed by* J^{no} Martin, *Printer to*
" *the Society.*

" BROUNCKER, Pres."

" It having happened to me some years
" past to have been deeply engaged in this
" same consideration of the alphabet, by a
" *worthy designe of giving relief* to a *deaf*
" and *dumb* person in the year 1659, re-
" commended to my care, and being at last
" prevailed with by divers persons, who
" remember *the success* of that enterprize,
" to communicate the way and method I
" *then used*, I have adventured to publish
" my thoughts concerning the nature of
" letters, more in respect of the Appendix,

" or application of them to *that excellent*
" *purpofe*, &c."

Pref. to Elem. of Speech, by *Holder.*

" But the chief defign here intended by
" this account of the *natural* alphabet, is
" to prepare a more eafie and expedite
" way to inftruct fuch as are *deaf and*
" *dumb*, and dumb onely by confequence
" of the want of hearing (by fhewing
" them the proper figures of the motions
" of the organs, whereby letters are framed)
" to be able to pronounce all letters and
" fyllables and words, and in a good mea-
" fure, *to difcern them by the eye*, when
" pronounced by an other.—And although
" this cannot be directly and immediately
" taught and learnt, *as to every particular*
" *letter* of the alphabet (as will be fuffi-
" ciently manifeft in the enfuing difcourfe)
" yet he who has this exact knowledge of
" of

"of the nature and difference of letters,
"by knowing withal *what can be done*, and
"what cannot be immediately performed,
"will be able to pursue such an attempt
"with steadiness, and having made his first
"progress in what is obvious and fesible,
"will then (without expence of *fruitless*
"labour) proceed to seek out and *invent*
"*other ways* to compass about and accom-
"plish his designed effect.

"And by these ways (as *I myself have
"made some experiment*) it is *not impossible*,
"no, nor very difficult to be done, even
"in those who were born *deaf* and *dumb*."
Holder's Elem. of Speech, pp. 15, 16.

"Neither did any such hopes or ambi-
"tion" (as those of rectifying *alphabets*
universally) "set my thoughts on work,
"but partly the *worthiness and curiosity* of
"this subject in itself, and chiefly the

"great

"great ufe of an accurate knowledge of
"the nature of letters, and fpeech, in di-
"recting to a fteady and *effectual way of*
"*inftructing deaf and dumb* perfons, to obtain a
"reafonable perfection of *utterance of fpeech,*
"and to difcern (in fome meafure) with
"their eye, by obferving the motions of
"the mouth, what others fpeak: and to
"that end, I have added to this Effay an
"Appendix relating that defign, both
"which I hope and promife myfelf, will
"find a candid reception, from thofe who
"fhall confider thefe poor and flight pa-
"pers, as a work of *charity* and compaf-
"fion, and may be acceptable to them, as
"it is pleafing to myfelf, to have ftudied
"relief for the calamitous and deplorable
"condition of perfons *deaf* and *dumb*."

Holder's Elements, pp. 109, 110.

"Now

"Now as to the moſt general caſe of thoſe who are deaf and dumb, I ſay, they are dumb by *conſequence* from their deafneſs, *onely becauſe they are not taught to ſpeak.*—The natural part of ſpeech, viz. words made of letters by ſuch exquiſite various articulations, is *learnt by much practice and imitation*; and much more the *artificial* part, viz. *inſtitution of ſignificancy of language,* cannot be acquired without great help of inſtruction: and to that end, the tong and ear, ſpeaking and hearing, hold a correſpondence, by which *we* learn to imitate the ſound of ſpeech, and underſtand the meaning of it: but he that *never hears* a word ſpoken, nor can be told what it ſignifies, it is no wonder, if ſuch an one remain ſpeechleſs: as out of queſtion *any one muſt do* (though of integral principles) who from an infant ſhould be bred up among

"among *mutes*, and have no teaching.
"Such then is the case in hand, that they
"who want that *sence* of *discipline* (hear-
"ing) are also by consequence deprived of
"speech, not by any immediate *organical*
"*indisposition*, but for want of *discipline*.—
"Finding then a person in this condition, *not*
"*capable of hearing*, if we would endeavour
"to make use of the organs of speech
"(supposed to be of sufficient constitution)
"there is no way, but to have recourse to
"the other learned sense, which is *seeing*,
"and to find out some means (although
"farther about, and more laborious) of
"instructing him *by his eyes*, and shewing
"him the visible motions and figures of
"the mouth, by which speech is articu-
"lated; and to apply the doctrine of
"letters to this use and purpose is the de-
"sign of this Appendix, where our first
"business had need to be to animate the
"under-

"undertaker, and confider whether it be
"poffible or no; for it muft confeffed,
"that there lie in the way great objections
"and difficulties, which *feem to difcourage*,
"and portend fuch a defign unfefible:—
"but I doubt not to fhew you, how to
"overcome thofe feeming demonftrable
"impoffibilities, and fhew how truely it is
"faid, *venit miferis folertia rebus.*"

Holder's *Appendix* concerning Perfons
Deaf and Dumb, pp. 115, 116.

Then intervene fome general rules of proceeding, ufed and recommended by him (Dr. Holder) which are omitted for brevity's fake.

"It is obfervable, that the hiftories of
"thofe who could difcern *fpeech* by their
"*eye* are, *moft* of fuch as having had knowledge of language, and a readinefs in
"fpeaking,

"speaking, falling afterwards into *deaf-*
"*ness*, have loft the *use* of speech, but
"still retein the memory of it: now if we
"can by induftry make any deaf and dumb
"perfon *reasonably perfect* in the language
"and pronunciation, he may alfo be capa-
"ble of the fame privilege of *underftand-*
"*ing by the eye* what is fpoken, though the
"letters *fingly pronounced* are ambiguous,
"and may deceive him: in fhort, though
"it be impoffible for a deaf perfon by his
"eye accurately and *certainly* to diftinguifh
"letters *fingly fpoken*, (as it is likewife in
"words equivocal, fpoken, and letters
"whifpered, *to thofe that hear*) yet in
"tract of fpeech, as a *dubious word* is
"eafily known by a coherence with the
"reft; and a dubious letter by the whole
"word, fo may a *deaf* perfon, having at-
"tained a competent knowledge of lan-
"guage, and affifted by an acute fagacity,

"*by*

" *by some more evident* word discovered
" by his eye, *know* the sense, and *by*
" *the* sence, other words, and by the
" words the obscurer letters, and so, not-
" withstanding this difficulty objected, make
" good use of this institution, *not onely to*
" *speak*, but in a good measure (so far as
" to serve for converse) know what others
" say to him: and the rather because hav-
" ing learnt by his eye, and being inured
" to that kind of observation, he is quicker
" to perceive the motions of articulation and
" conjunctures of letters in words, *than we*
" *can easily* imagine.—Having thus sur-
" mounted the difficulties, I shall mention
" some such things as give *encouragement*
" to this enterprize: and first, that which
" was before hinted, that in deaf and dumb
" persons, their *necessity* excites a great ob-
" servation and *sagacity*, to supply their
" defects, and to bear up, and maintain
" converse

"converse with others who enjoy the be-
"nefit of all their senses. And being de-
"nyed communication by the *ear*, their
"*eyes* are the more vigilant, attent, and
"heedful, which renders them much more
"capable of being improved by directions
"and instructions applied to that sense;
"and gives a delight and encouragement to
"those who teach such *apprehensive* scho-
"lars." Ibidem, pp. 125—128.

"Language being defined *a connexion of*
"*the best signes for communication*, and
"written language *visible signes* of the
"signes audible: and the *elements* of each
"respectively, and the *correspondence* and mu-
"tual assistance of each to the other, being
"such, as in the foregoing discourse is
"more fully shewn; you have a great
"help, by *shewing* letters and words *writ-*
"*ten*, to conduct a deaf person on, in ex-
"ercising

"ercifing him to exprefs the fame by pro-
"nunciation, and whatfoever you gain
"upon him *this* way will be reteined, and
"made ufe of in the other: add to this
"the *admirable* curiofity, and *fingular excel-*
"*lency* of the defign, the confideration where-
"of will fuftein the patience, and animate
"the induftry of him who fhall undertake
"it.—Having thus confidered what ground
"and encouragement there may be for
"fuch an undertaking: I fhall now, in
"the plaineft manner I can, lay down fuch
"*directions* and *rules*, as *I myfelf have* made
"trial of to *inftruct a deaf perfon* to make
"ufe of his *organs of fpeech*, and *ceafe to*
"*be dumb*, enjoying the great felicity of
"that moft expedite way of communica-
"tion; which may ferve till *fome more able*
"*perfon* fhall be excited by improvements
"and additions to give *a greater perfection*
                        "to

" to this defigne :—firſt make your *own* al-
" phabet, &c." Ibid. pp. 131, 2.

Then follows *his particular method,* which is omitted alſo.

" Now befides thefe directions already
" given, you will find when you come
" to practife, that your own earneſtneſs
" and contention to effect what you are
" about, will, continually, whileſt you
" are at work with him, fuggeſt to you fe-
" veral artifices, whereby to make him
" better apprehend what you would have
" him pronounce, *which cannot* fo well be
" tho't of, beforehand, *nor rules fet down*
" *for it in writing.*

" Now when the labour and patience of
" getting the alphabet is over, the main
" difficulty is overcome. — Having thus
" made

" made him learn the alphabet, and the
" characters of it, next, (or together with
" the other) teach him an alphabet upon
" his fingers, or several parts of his hands,
" by placing the letters there, which you
" may devise at pleasure."—For example,
" particularly, let the extremity of the
" thumb and four fingers of the left-hand
" (when any of them is pointed at by the
" forefinger of the *right* hand, or by any
" kind of fescue) signify the vowels *a,*
" *e, i, o, u,*"—&c. &c. p. 151.

" I had once in my thoughts to contrive
" a method of Grammar and Dictionary
" for this use: of grammar, more than I
" can now comprise in short hints: and the
" latter alphabetically, containing the words
" of the language which the *deaf* person is
" to learn; as suppose English: and the
" ex-

" expofition being a reprefentation of the
" figure of fo many words as can be de-
" fcribed; and of the reft by fuch other
" fignes as might be thought of, referring the
" fynonimas to thofe which have expofitions;
" by which he might help himfelf to
" know the meaning of fuch words, as he
" fhould meet with, and by often looking
" on it gain the knowledge of words: but
" the occafion of exciting and exercifing
" my thoughts being unhappily removed,
" I went no further; but hope to fee them
" perfected, by thofe who fhall meet with
" fuch like occafions: and indeed fuch a
" work as this, is not to be perfected by
" ftudy alone, but muft and will receive
" many hints and helps, and to be thought
" on otherwife, whilft the endeavour is ex-
" cited, being under *experiment* and *prac-*
" *tice:* but fo far as I had occafion to ftudy,
" and *practife with happy fuccefs*, I have
" faith-

"faithfully imparted, and wish it may be useful to those who stand in need of it." Holder's Appendix to Elem. of Speech, pp. 156, 7, 8.

Thirdly—Extract * *(and translation)* of a letter of the ingenious Dr. *John Wallis*, (one of the first promoters of the Institution of the Royal Society) to Dr. *Thomas Beverley, reprinted* 1765 in Latin, annexed to his Latin Grammar of the English Language, and entitled

* Extracted from the *Latin* publication, for the more particular satisfaction of foreigners.

" Epistola

" Epistola ad D. Thomam Beverley, de *mutis*,

" *surdisque* informandis.

" Sept. xxx. 1698.

" Clarissime Vir,

" Literas tuas Sept. 22, datas, post ali-
" quot dies accepi. Quibus *casum* narras
" familiæ cujusdam (cui tu notus) *vere*
" *plorandum*, quod ex *octo* liberis jam viven-
" tibus, *quinque* sunt plane *muti, surdique*
" (& quidem ideo, ni fallor, *muti*, quia
" *surdi*). Petis, ut velim tibi indicare,
" quibus modis, possit his defectibus optime
" subveniri.—Quippe qui noveris (quod
" intelligo) D. *Alexandrum Popham* (adhuc
" ni fallor in vivis) quem *(surdum natum)*
" docueram ego, (jam ante annos quasi 34
" aut 35) *distincte loqui* (utut metuo, ne
" istius aliquid quadantenus jam fuerit
" oblitus:) atque sermonem loquelarem ea-
" tenus intelligere, ut potuerit animi sua
" sensa *(mediocriter)* scripto insinuare, at-
" que

"VOX OCULIS SUBJECTA."

Translation.

"Letter to Dr. Beverley, &c.

"Honoured Sir,

"Your letter of the 22d September, I received some days ago, in which you relate a truely deplorable case of a certain family (of your acquaintance) that out of *eight* children now living, *five* are absolutely *deaf* and *dumb* (and indeed *dumb*, unless I mistake, *because deaf*.)—
"You request, that I would shew you, by what means, these defects may best be remedied.—For you know (as I understand) Dr. *Alexander Popham* (who is still living, if I mistake not) whom *(being born deaf)* I had taught, (now about 34 or 35 years since,) to *speak distinctly* (although I fear lest something of it may have been now in a measure forgotten) and so far to understand common dis-

"course

" que ab aliis sibi scripta intelligere: quod
" & ante feceram de *D. Daniele Whaley*
" (jam nuper mortuo) qui fuerat inde a
" puero *surdus*.—Aliis aliquot qui non fue-
" rint surdi, sed ita linguis impedita, ut
" vel plane balbutirent, & loquendo titu-
" barent, aut literas saltem aliquas, vel
" non omnino, vel non nisi hæsitantem
" proferre possent, docui distincte & ex-
" pedite proferre sonos illos, quos ante non
" potuerant: ita ut difficultatem illam vel
" plane superaverint, vel ita, saltem ut vix
" discerni posset.—Alios aliquot surdos
" loquelam docere non aggressus sum: sed
" solummodo ut res scriptas mediocriter
" intelligerent, suaque sensa scripto qua-
" dantenus, insinuarent: qui tempore non
" longo progressus eos fecerint, rerumque
" plurimarum notitiam acquisiverint, multo
" ultra quam quod putabatur fieri posse a
" quoquam in eorum circumstantiis posito
" fuerintque

" courſe, that he could communicate his
" thoughts in writing (tolerably well) and
" comprehend what was written from
" others to himſelf. Which alſo I had,
" before, done by Dr. *Daniel Whaley*
" (lately dead) who had been deaf from
" the time he was a boy.—Some others,
" who were *not deaf*, but had ſuch impe-
" diments in ſpeech, that they either ab-
" ſolutely heſitated and ſtammered in ſpeak-
" ing, or could not utter ſome letters, at
" all, ſcarcely, or at leaſt not without ſtut-
" tering, I have taught *diſtinctly*, and *readily*
" to produce thoſe ſounds which before they
" could not; ſo that they fully overcame that
" difficulty, or ſo far as that it could ſcarcely
" be perceived. Some other *deaf* perſons I did
" *not* go the length of teaching *ſpeech*, but
" only that they might underſtand, tolerably,
" things that were written, and could com-
" municate in ſome degree, in *writing*, their
" own thoughts: who, in no long time, might
" make

" fuerintque *plane capaces* acquirendi (si
" plenius exculti) *ulteriorem cognitionem* quæ
" posset scripto impertiri.

" Priorem hujus pensi partem (nempe ut
" doceantur loqui si prius muti, aut expe-
" dite loqui si prius hæsitantur) expedire
" soleo, indicando, quo situ motuque dis-
" ponenda sunt guttur, lingua, labia, cæ-
" teraque loquendi organa, pro singulis re-
" spective sonis, inter loquendum adhiberi
" solitis: quippe, his rite dispositis, spi-
" ritus ex pulmone afflatus, eos formabit
" sonos, sive se audiat, sive non audiat,
" qui sic profert.

" De

" make that progress, and might acquire
" the knowledge of many things, *much*
" *beyond* what might be thought possible to
" be done by any one in their circum-
" stances, and have been *fully capable* (if
" *more* cultivated) of acquiring the *greatest*
" *degree of knowledge* which can possibly be
" *imparted* by writing.

" The first part of this task (as they *may*
" *be* taught to speak, *if before dumb,* or
" *readily to speak* if before with impedi-
" ments) I use to forward, by shewing by
" what position and motion, the parts of
" the throat, the tongue, lips, and other
" organs of speech, are to be disposed for
" each of the *sounds* respectively, wont to
" be applied in speaking. For by the right
" disposition of these, the breath being expel-
" led from the lungs, he who thus produced
" it, *will form those sounds,* whether *he doth*
" *or doth doth not, hear them.*

"De hac sonorum omnium loquelarium formatione respectiva, distinctam ego dudum tradidi rationem (omnium credo primus qui hoc aggressi sunt) in Tractatu de Loquela (præfixo meæ de Lingua Anglicana Grammaticæ) anno 1653 primum edito. Atque hac fretus origine *Whaleum* primo, deinde *Pophamum* docui, voces quasvis cujusvis linguæ distincte proferre (saltem quas *ipse possem* pronunciare); et quidem Polonicarum difficillimas (domino Polono, qui aderat, exigente, factumque comprobante, & admirante): exterosque docui, sonos nostros expedite proferre, quos ipsi sibi senserint impossibiles.—Estque hæc duarum brevior pars operis (utut censeri soleat magis stupenda). Verum hæc, absque rel quæ, non magno foret usui. Nam, verba tantum proferre, psittacorum instar, ignorato interim quid significent haud vitæ commodis inserviret.", &c. &c.

"Sed

"Of this respective formation of all the lo-
"quelary sounds, I have some time ago given a
"distinct account (the first of any one, I be-
"lieve, who attempted it) in a Treatise of
"Speech, prefixed to my Grammar of the
"English Language, first published in the
"year 1653: and relying on this begin-
"ning, I first taught *Whaley,* then *Popham,*
"distinctly to utter any words whatever (*even
"as I myself could pronounce*) and indeed the
"most difficult of the Polish, (to the ap-
"probation and admiration of a certain
"Polish lord who came to prove the fact,)
"and I have taught *foreigners* readily to
"pronounce *our* sounds, which they them-
"selves had thought impossible.—And this
"part of the work is but the shorter of
"the two (howsoever it may be imagined
"the most astonishing). But this, without
"the rest, would be of little use.—For to
"pronounce words only, like parrots, being
"still

"Sed reliqua pars operis (ut *fcripti* fer-
"monis ufus habeatur) eft id quod tu
"quæris.—In ordine ad hunc fermonis
"ufum, eft imprimis neceffarium ut mutus
"(informandus) difcat fcribere, quo fit quod
"oculo repræfentet, id quod fonus (literá-
"rum) folet auribus exhibere.—Erit de-
"inde valde commodum (quia penna cum
"atramento non femper præfto eft) ut do-
"ceatur, quo pacto poffit fingulas literas
"defignare (puta fitu motuve digiti, ma-
"nus, aliufve partis corporis) quod loco
"fit fcriptæ literæ; verbi gratia, ut quin-
"que vocales *a, e, i, o, u,* notentur apici-
"bus quinque digitorum; reliquæ literæ
"*b, c, d,* &c. alio fitu motuve, ut commo-
"dum videatur, et ex pacto conveniat.—

"Poftea,

" ſtill ignorant of their ſignification, would
" not ſerve for the purpoſes of life."

Pp. 267, 8, 9.

" But the remaining part of the work, that
" he may attain the uſe of *written language*,
" is that which you ſeek.—In order to this
" uſe of language, it is in the firſt place ne-
" ceſſary, that the *dumb* perſon (to be in-
" ſtructed) ſhould learn to *write*, by
" which means may be repreſented to *the*
" *eye*, that which the ſound (of letters)
" is uſed to exhibit *to the ears:* it will
" then be very convenient (as pen and ink
" is not always at hand) that he ſhould be
" taught in what manner each of the *letters*
" *may be ſignified* (ſuppoſe by the poſition
" and motion of the finger, hand, or any
" other part of the body) which may be
" in ſtead of *written letters*. For example,
" that the five vowels may be noted by the

" ends

" Postea, *docendus est sermo, eadem methodo,*
" qua pueri solent linguam ediscere (quam
" forte plurimi vix animadvertunt): cum
" hoc saltem discrimine; pueri sonos aure
" discunt: mutus signa (eorum sonorum
" indicia) *discit oculo.* Sunt autem tum
" hæc, tum illi, pariter ad placitum signi-
" ficantia, earundem sive rerum, sive no-
" tionum.

" Atque ut pueri solent primum discere
" rerum nomina; sic commodum est, huic
" muto, gradatim suppeditare nomenclatu-
" ram; qua contineantur aliquam multa
" nomina rerum passim occurentium &
" oculo obviarium, (ut indicari possint
" res

" ends of the five fingers: the other letters
" *b, c, d,* &c. by other positions and mo-
" tion, as may seem convenient, and as
" may be agreed.—Afterwards he is to be
" taught speech, *by the same method,* which
" boys use to learn a language (which
" perhaps very many have scarcely ever
' thought of) with this difference alone,
" children in general learn *sounds by the*
" *ear,* a dumb person learns *signs* (which
" are images of those sounds) *by the eye:*
" for both those, as well as these, are
" equally significant, *at pleasure,* either of
" things or of ideas.

" And as boys are wont *at first* to learn
" the names of things, so it is convenient,
" to supply this mute person by degrees,
" with a vocabulary, in which let there be
" contained any number of names of things
" commonly occurring and obvious to the
   " eyes,

" res his nominibus respondentes.) Quæ no-
" mina commodo ordine sint disposita, sub va-
" riis titulis; non confuse, sed eo ordine, si-
" tuque distributa (per varias columnas
" aliasve debitas in charta positiones,) ita ut
" ipso situ suo insinuent oculo quam inter
" se respectum habeant res his nominibus
" indicatæ. Verbi gratia: ut contraria
" vel correlativa, oppositis chartæ partibus
" scribantur; subordinata, seu appendicula,
" principalibus subjecta. Quod memoriæ
" localis (quæ dicitur) vicem quadantenus
" suppleat.—Sic *v. g.* in una chartula, sub
" titulo *mankind* (homo) scribantur (non
" confuse sed commodo situ) *man, woman,*
" *child* (boy, girl); atque si libet, nomina
" quorundam in familia, aut alibi cogni-
" torum, relictis locis vacuis; pro nominibus
" aliis, vocabulisque cogeneris naturæ infe-
" rendis, prout occasio tulerit.—Tum, in
" alia chartula, sub titulo *body* (corpus)
" scri-

"eyes, so that the things may be shewn accord-
"ding to these names, and placed in con-
"venient order, under various heads; not
"confusedly, but in that method, and so
"distributed in situation (by various co-
"lumns, and other proper positions on
"the paper) that the things indicated may
"communicate by their situation, to his
"*eye*, the relation which they have to
"those names.—For instance, let contrary
"things, or correlatives, be wrote upon
"*opposite* parts of the paper.—Subordinate
"things, or appendages, be placed *under*
"their principals, which may answer in
"some measure the end of a local memory
"(as it is called). Thus, for example, on
"a little piece of paper, *under* the head or
"title *mankind*, let there be wrote (not
"irregularly, but in a convenient situation)
"*man, woman, child (boy, girl)*, and if
"you please, the names of any body in
"the

"scribantur (situ item commodo) *head,*
"face, forehead, eye, &c. &c. &c.

P. 270.

" the family, or of other acquaintance,
" leaving vacant places, for inferting other
" names, and terms of the fame nature,
" according as occafion fhall offer.—Then,
" on a little piece of paper, *under* the title
" *body*, let there be wrote (in the fame
" convenient and proper fituation) *head*,
" *face*, forehead, eye," &c. &c.

P. 270.

The continuation of thefe directions, confifting of examples, of many of the objects of nature, animate and inanimate, and each fpecies under its refpective genus, together with an ingenious Compendium of a fuitable Grammar or Accidence, ufed by Dr. Wallis, is all here omitted, for the reafons before given.—The following paragraph therefore will clofe the quotations from this author.

" And

"Et quidem, si mutus ille surdusque, sit,
"alias, bonæ indolis; et qui docet, justæ
"sagacitatis, poterit hic tali methodo (gra-
"datim procedendo, cum debita tum do-
"centis, tum discentis diligentia) intra
"unius quasi anni spatium (expertus lo-
"quor) majores progressus observare, quam
"quis expectaverit; bonaque jacta fun-
"damenta ulterioris institutionis, sive in
"rebus religionis, sive aliis eruditionis
"partibus, quæ legendo possint obtineri."
Epistola D. Wallisii ad D. Tho. Beverley, pp. 279, 80.

Fourthly—Quotation or extract from the celebrated Dr. *Amman* of Amsterdam.
"*Dissertatio de Loquela.*"
Anno Dom. 1700.

"Nec tamen diu ibi commoratus; *viri*
"*amicissimi* precibus *Harlemum* redire lu-
"bens

" VOX OCULIS SUBJECTA."

" And indeed, if the *deaf* and *dumb*
" perfon be otherwife of good capacity,
" and the *teacher* of *proper* fagacity, *he may*
" *by* fuch a method as this (proceeding
" gradually, with *due* diligence both of
" the learner and teacher) *within the space*
" even of a year, (I fpeak by experience)
" make greater progrefs than any one could
" expect: and good foundations be laid for
" the greatest degree of education, either in
" matters of religion, or in *other parts of*
" *learning,* which *can possibly be obtained by*
" reading.

Letter of Dr. Wallis, to Dr. T. Beverley,
pp. 279, 80.

Tranflation.
" Amman's *Treatife* on *Speech*.
" Neither did I long abide there, for I
" was willingly conftrained by the entreaties
" of

" bens adigebar, *filiæ* ipsius *surda*, & ob-
" surditatem connatam, *mutæ*, erudiendi
" gratia : quem scopum plus fere quam at-
" tigi, & eventus meum patrisque spem
" longe superavit. *venustissima* enim ista
" *puella* angusto duorum mensium spatio
" non tantum satis articulate legebat, sed
" & quævis tarde pronunciata in chartam
" conjiciebat : jam autem de quacunque re
" non inepte confabulatur; alios *surdæ*
" licet loquentis oculis audit; & ad inter-
" rogata promte respondet.

" Tandem *methodum*, qua hæc omnia
" illam docui, non indignam judicavi, quæ
" in proximi emolumentum, sub nomine
" *surdæ*

"of a *most friendly man* to return to *Har-*
"*lem*, for the fake of inftructing a *deaf*
"*daughter* of his, who, having been born
"*deaf*, was alfo *dumb*, which purpofe I almoft
"more than effected, and the fuccefs far
"furpaffed my own hopes, as well as thofe
"of her father; for that *charming girl*
"in the fhort fpace of two months could
"not only read tolerably plain, but alfo
"take down on paper any words flowly
"pronounced: fhe now converfes, not amifs,
"on any fubject; and, although deaf, fhe
"hears with her eyes what others fpeak,
"and replies readily to interrogations.

"At length, I have judged the *method*
"by which I taught her all thefe things
"not unworthy to be publifhed, for the
"benefit of a neighbor, under the title of
"*Surdus Loquens,* or the *Deaf Speaking,*

"*surdi loquentis*, publica fieret, doctiorum
"judiciis ulterius trutenanda."
    Dedicatio ad *Johannem Hudde*, Dissertatio
      de Loquela.

    "*Candido Lectori Præfatio*.
"Nova tibi & forsan incredibilis, videbitur
"B. L. hæc nostra de instituendis *surdis* doc-
"trina, non tamen inaudita est; fuerunt enim,
"ut dudum accepi, quidam, quibus eadem
"cura fuit: qui autem ii fuerint, & quid
"effecerint, hactenus me latuit, sancteque
"testor, mihi, antequam ipse excogitaram,
"ne vestigium ejus apud ullum *auctorem*
"occurrisse.—Cum sexto, ni fallor, surdo
"erudiendo operam darem, familiariter
"nosse mihi contigit illustrum illum philo-
"sophum Fr. Merc. Van Helmont, τοῦ
                                   "υἱὸν

"in order to be more thoroughly examined by judges of more learning."

Dedication (of *Treatise on Speech*) to John Hudde, conful of Amsterdam, 1700.

"Amman's *Preface to the Reader.*

"New and incredible as this art of ours of inſtructing the deaf may ſeem to you, courteous reader, it is neverthelefs *not unheard* of: for there have been certain perſons, as I have lately underſtood, who have had the ſame purſuits: who they were, and what they have effected, hath hitherto been unknown to me, and I ſolemnly declare, before I myſelf employed my thoughts thereon, never to have met with the trace of it in any author whatever. When I had inſtructed the ſixth *deaf perſon* (if I miſtake not) I happened to be familiarly acquainted with that celebrated philoſopher F. M. *Van Helmont, now among the ſaints*, who "gave

" νῦν ἐν ἁγίοις, qui ante plures annos
" *Alphabetum quoddam naturale* a se edi-
" tum narrabat, ubi de *surdorum natorum*
" informatione se egisse testabatur: cum
" autem me instituentem videret & audi-
" ret, non modo me sibi nihil debere, sed,
" ut erat summa *viri* ingenuitas, *se longe a*
" *me superatum in praxi fatebatur.* Verum
" dum hæc de loquela dissertatio sub prælo
" erat, eodem fere tempore, & incidi in
" locum eruditissimi *P. Zachiæ* quæst. me-
" dico-legal. Lib. II. Tit. ii. Quæst. viii. n.
" 7. ubi ex *Vallesio*, Lib. de Sac. Philosoph.
" cap. 3. narrat de *Monacho* qui *surdos* a
" nativitate loqui docebat, preterea nihil
" addit: & redditæ mihi sunt literæ, a
" viro clariss. *Jo. Wallis*, Mathemat. Oxonii
" Professore ad me exaratæ, quibus se ea,
" quæ in *surdo meo loquente* tradideram, non
" modo tentasse, sed feliciter olim pere-
 " gisse

"gave me an account of a *certain natural*
"*alphabet* published many years ago by
"him, in which publication he declares to
"have attempted the information of the
"*deaf born*, but when he saw and heard
"me teaching, he not only confessed that
"I owed nothing to him, but with the
"highest ingenuousness acknowledged him-
"self *very far exceeded by me in practice.*—
"But while this Treatise on Speech was
"in the press, I accidentally fell in with
"the passage of the very learned *P. Za-*
"*chia's* Quæst. Medico-legal, Lib. II. Tit.
"ii. Quæst. viii. n. 7. where, (out of *Val-*
"*lesius*, Lib. de Sac. Philosoph. chap. 3.)
"he tells of *Monachus*, who taught those
"*deaf* from their nativity to speak, but
"says nothing farther; and almost at the
"very same time, letters were delivered
"addressed to me from the celebrated *John*
"*Wallis*, Professor of Mathematicks at Ox-
"ford,

" giffe mihi fignificabat, quafque cum re-
" fponfo ad eas dato, ne Æfopicæ inftar
" cornicis alienis fuperbire plumis viderer
" Præfationis loco hic inferere volui, quo fibi
" B. L. innotefceret, quid mihi cum tanto
" viro fit commune, & in quibus ab eo dif-
" feram."—Præfatio ad Lectorem.

" Verum graviffimæ huic calamitati pro
" cumulo accedit, quod omnem refpuere
" medicinam hactenus unanimiter, quan-
" tum fcio, fuerit credita, & propterea in-
" fanibilium numero adfcripta: at ego, re
" ferio mecum penfitata, *mutorum* plerof-
" que, quamvis *loquelæ organa* haberent
" fana,

"ford, in which he acquainted me that he
"had not only tried, but happily accom-
"plished formerly thofe very things which
"I had publifhed in my book, called *Sur-
"dus Loquens*, which letters, together with
"my anfwer thereto, left I fhould feem,
"like Æfop's crow, to be proud of others
"wings, I have refolved to infert in this
"Preface, by which it may become known
"what I had in common with fo great a
"man, and in what I differed from him."

Amman's Preface to the Reader.

"But the weight of this heavy calamity
"is encreafed, in as much as (fo far as I
"know) it hath hitherto been univerfally
"fuppofed to bid defiance to every re-
"medy, and accordingly ranked among
"the incurable evils: but I have tho-
"roughly and ferioufly confidered the fub-
"ject, and have obferved that the moft part
"of

"sana, talis esse, animadverti, quod simul
"& *surdi* essent, quare *surditatem* quidem
"medelam admittter penitus desperavi,
"de *loquela* autem plane aliter sensi. *Sermo*
"enim humanus, ut cuivis cum paulo at-
"tentius mecum contemplanti patebit, est
"mistura quædam plurimorum diversi ge-
"neris sonorum, quorum varietas, dictante
"id ratione, variis organorum quorundum
"motibus a me tribuebatur, quos modo
"satis visibiles forent, sufficere arbitrabar,
"ut *surdi* eos oculis, non secus ac cæteri
"*sonos ipsos* auribus discernerent, & ita
"*loqui* tandem discerent.—Primum rei peri-
"culum ipse coram speculo in me feci,
"eamque statim & utilem & possibilem ju-
                               "dicavi

"of those who have been *dumb*, although they have the organs of speech perfect, were such as were also *deaf*; wherefore, although indeed I have altogether despaired of *deafness* receiving a remedy, I have been of a very different opinion respecting *speech*. For human language, as will appear to any one who will attentively consider it a little with me, is a certain compound of many sounds, of different kinds, whose variety, as reason suggests, is by me attributed to the *various motions* of particular organs, which being sufficiently visible, I was satisfied that the deaf might discern those *motions*, by the *eyes*, in like manner as others discern the *sounds* themselves by their *ears*, and so might learn at length to speak.— I made the first trial of the matter upon myself, before a looking-glass, and forthwith judged it both useful and practicable,

"dicavi, non minorem videns inter motus
"istos differentiam, quam inter sonos ipsos
"& characteres eas exprimentes, ex eoque
"tempore *surdum* aliquem erudiendum op-
"tavi. Amici quibus mentem aperui,
"quosque, ut mihi in quærendo *discipulo*
"operam darent rogavi, me velut insanum
"*mathematicum* risere, brevi tamen mutata
"sententia, cum discipulum illis paulo post
"& *loquentem* & legentem sisterem. Fracta
"igitur glacie non prius destiti, quam
"tantum negocium ad prepositum finem
"perduxerim, *surdorumque* sortem, *Divino*
"*adspirante Numine*, non modo reddiderim
"tolerabiliorem, sed, et vulgari in eo præ-
"stantiorem, sicut *exempla* testantur, quod
"alios, voce etiam maxime submissa lo-
"quentes, intelligant, aures suas in oculis
gerendo.

"cable, not seeing less difference between "those *motions* than between the *sounds* "themselves and the characters expressing "them, and from that time I wished to "have a *deaf* person to instruct. Friends "to whom I opened my mind, and those "whom I requested to procure a scholar "for me, laughed at me, as a mad mathe- "matician, or necromancer; they very "shortly, however, changed their opinion, "when, after a little while, I produced "to them a scholar, both *speaking* and *read-* "*ing*: having thus broke the ice, I did "not desist, untill I had brought the bu- "siness to the proposed end, and (*prompted* "*and encouraged by the Divine Being*) had "rendered the condition of the *deaf* not "only more tolerable, but even prefer- "able to the vulgar, (as *examples* witness) "*in that they* can understand others when "speaking, even in the very lowest voice,

"cat-

"gerendo.—*Methodi* qua id effeci, ſpecimen ante aliquot annos edidi, quo & exteri eam imitari poſſent," &c. &c.

Jo. Conrad. *Amman* " de Loquela," Amſtelodæmi, 1700, pp. 3, 4.

"carrying (as it were) their *ears* in their
"eyes.—A specimen of the *method* by
"which I effected it, I published some
"years ago, by which even foreigners may
"imitate it," &c. &c.

Amman's Treatise on Speech, entitled *Dissertatio de Loquela*, printed at Amsterdam, 1700, pp. 3, 4.

Fifthly.—Extract from *Herries*'s Elements of Speech.

"From a progress so simple as this, Dr.
"Amman informs us, that in a short time
"he taught several deaf pupils, *not only to
"write and speak* correctly; but to *under-
"stand* throughout what they had written
"and spoken. Nor did the curious art
"perish with him: it is practised at this
"present time *with great success.*—Among
"those who are engaged in this undertak-
"ing, *Mr. Braidwood* of Edinburgh is de-
"servedly eminent: It may be found,
"however, that those ingenious gentle-
"men pursue a plan, somewhat different
"from that of *Amman*, which I have now
"mentioned. Every master will adopt
"that method, which *by experience* he finds
"to be most effectual;—AN OBJECT SO
"CURIOUS AND IMPORTANT AS THIS, IS
"CERTAINLY ENTITLED TO THE WARM-
"EST

" EST ENCOURAGEMENT OF THE PUBLIC.
—If a person, who has been deprived
" from his infancy of the faculties of
" speech and hearing, can be taught *even to*
" *converse intelligibly*, it is *a wonderful* ac-
" quisition.—I am indeed apprehensive,
" that even with the utmost attention be-
" stowed upon him, he will scarcely be able
" to display any *gracefulness*, or harmony
" of utterance.—The *charms of modulation*
" are excited and directed by hearing
" alone. Notwithstanding this, I see no
" reason why a deaf person may not be
" taught from mechanical principles, to
" ascend the gradations of music. If by
" the sense of *feeling* he can discover a vo-
" cal from an unvocal sound, why may he
" not produce a high or low tone, by
" elevating or depressing the larynx?—
" After all, the nice *variation and melody*
" *of the voice*, may perhaps, to him, re-

" main

"main an impenetrable myſtery.—How grateful then ought thoſe to be to heaven, who enjoy, in its utmoſt perfection, that moſt valuable and enrapturing ſenſe of hearing! who can thence feel and imitate every air of muſic, and every modification of language!—We have now, by the moſt ſimple progreſs, endeavoured to unfold the curious *theory* of articulate ſounds: we have aſcertained their number, arranged them according to their different qualities, and deſcribed minutely the formation of each: We have likewiſe conſidered the letters or marks by which they are repreſented in writing. From theſe principles, we have offered ſome *hints*, with regard to the beſt method of *cultivating the voice* in children, and *removing* impediments in pronunciation, and of teaching *the dumb to ſpeak*." Herries' Elemen. pp. 78, 9, 80.

As

As the effects of well-attested practice are more likely to convince the generality of the world than a volume of reasonings, the preceding pages may be supposed to have removed every doubt, respecting the *possibility* of the art herein treated of, and even to satisfy the reader, that there *have been some* instances, in which considerable progress hath been made, heretofore, at various times, since the middle of the last century: the next thing proposed is to demonstrate that the wonderful art is *now* actually very *happily practised*, within this island. To some it may seem unnecessary, if not whimsical, to describe as *extraordinary, a school in this kingdom*; it may seem superfluous, especially, to adduce the same instance that others, (and authors of note in the literary world) have already, in their works: I would therefore observe, before I proceed, that notwithstanding,

each,

each, and either, have given a *satisfactory* although *concise* account of *Messrs. Braidwood's* Academy, yet, in the first place, it was not the original design of *their* publications, but was mentioned *(en passant)* only as a *curiosity* worthy of notice, and consequently, if their judicious and pertinent remarks on it are observed by any, it must be accidentally, in pursuit of *some other* information or amusement: Whereas to publish the utility of this Academy, in particular, with *their accounts* of it, *collectively, also,* is part of *the professed object* of this Essay; besides which, a *parent's* anxiety for an only and beloved son may well be supposed to create an interest, and stimulate to attentions, that cannot exist in any other breast, nor indeed be described by any words: another reason is, that mine were not only, *not mere visits of curiosity*, but were *not* short; the

first

first was near *six weeks*, the latter *four weeks*, during which, every day was devoted to the examination of the proficiency of my child, and of others in the same school, and of many days, I may say, *every hour* was *so devoted:* of course it will not be deemed vain or arrogant to assert, that none of the respectable characters beforementioned (quotations from whom are hereto annexed) could be supposed to have so minute, complete, and *incontestible* a knowledge of every circumstance as one who made it his business and pleasure for near ten weeks.

We shall therefore now come to the *second part of the title-page*, viz.

PART II.

A
PARTICULAR ACCOUNT
OF

The Academy of *Messrs. Braidwood* of Edinburgh *, (with concurrent Animadversions.)

THIS Academy is, in my opinion, to a speculative mind, one of the most interesting and wonderful objects in the world, regarded merely as a *philosophical curiosity*.

---

* I understand (since the commencement of this) from Mr. B., that, by the advice of many respectable characters, he has in contemplation to remove his Academy to the vicinity of the metropolis of this island.

To realize (without mature consideration) that those who *never heard* a sound, and still *continue deaf*, should be capable of uttering articulate expressions, with *grammatical accuracy*; of chusing the most proper words to convey their ideas, both in speech, and in written language; and not only so, but " *to hear with the eye,*" or (in other words) to be so acquainted with the various positions of the organs of speech, as to be enabled *(generally)* to know what is spoken by another, only by looking steadily at the countenance of the speaker, is really so difficult, and astonishing, that the incredulity of the world, herein, is not much to be wondered at.—All this, however, I myself have been actually (with raptures) a witness to;—I say, *generally* they understand what is said, because it is impossible to *know infallibly :*—They must *sometimes* mistake, many words of various significations being

being uttered, or articulated with nearly the same action of the organs (as for instance *ship* and *sheep*): The occurrence also of equivocal words is very frequent in discourse; which, if unconnected with others, the sense cannot be determined *absolutely* even by *those who hear*; but, as other words in a sentence explain the meaning and application of such equivocal words, as *vain, vein, vane,—write, right, rite,* and many others, so these deaf persons, if they can discern one single articulation, will by a peculiar quickness of sight and apprehension, and *long practice*, be able to rectify any mistake, or doubt, in the adjoining syllables, by connecting them in their mind: the labials or lip-consonants, for example, B, P, M [*], are very hard to

---

[*] Mr. *Sheridan,* in his useful Lectures on the Art of Reading, exhibits a *Scheme of the Alphabet,* in which he makes M a *nasal* consonant, p. 51;—but *Holder* calls it a naso-dental *labial.*

discriminate with the eye, being formed by nearly the same motion, or appulse of the lips, with only this difference that M occasions a visible contraction of the muscles of the *nose*. Suppose either should, at first, be taken for the other, yet being after a time perfectly acquainted with the component parts of every word, reading also in the countenance of the speaker, and knowing the other words or sentences, the general import of the subject-matter, they are seldom at a loss to ascertain which of the labial consonants * are used, and so likewise in other cases.—It is not, however, as of a mere philosophical curiosity, but of an *art* of the greatest *utility*, that an account is now given.

---

* The beforementioned respectable author of Lectures on the Art of Reading, makes V and F *mere* labials; whereas (as *Holder* calls them) they are (as I conceive) *labio-dentals*, or formed by the joint operation of *lips* and *teeth*.

Like

Like every thing elfe (however great) this Academy hath gradually been enlarged and eftablifhed from very fmall beginnings. *Mr. Braidwood*, the fenior profeffor, firft engaged in this undertaking with *one pupil*, in the year 1760.—As the *practical* part of the art was then new to himfelf, he confequently made comparatively flow progrefs, but he brought that pupil to *a great degree* of accomplifhment, (in a few years) in fpeaking and writing; and fome of his genuine compofitions in poetry, which I have feen, are *excellent*.— He augmented his number by degrees, and improved his method: his prefent coadjutor, or partner, *Mr. John Braidwood*, hath been in the practice with him, now about thirteen years, and being a *young* gentleman of *abilities* alfo, and great *application*, there is reafon to hope, if his life fhould be fpared, that many improvements upon his

pre-

predeceffor's inventions and practice, suggested by experience, will yet be made in this ingenious method: as, according to the common courfe of nature, he may be expected to furvive Mr. Braidwood, who hath often acknowledged to me, that his fuccefs, in confequence of new difcoveries made *in the courfe of teaching*, hath greatly exceeded what was at firft his higheft, or moft fanguine expectation:—Their number of fcholars at prefent (of both fexes) amounts to near twenty, including feveral who have only *impediments* in fpeech, without being deaf.—Thefe are all lodged and boarded under the fame roof with the teachers; and have all poffible attention paid to their health and comfort.—The apartments for the lads or boys being feparate, and at a diftance from thofe of the young women or girls.

As

As soon as they rise in the morning, they *all* repair to the same school-room, for an hour or two before breakfast.—A certain time is allowed of each day for *recreation*, in which the tutors are generally as much engaged and employed as while in school.—On *Sundays* they are exercised in *moral* and *religious* subjects during the forenoon.

This number consists of various ages from five to upwards of twenty years, but these gentlemen have instructed several others who did not begin until *more advanced* ages: those, however, who are taken in hand when *young*, before the organs grow stiff and rigid, (for want of use) generally *speak* most plainly, and pleasantly.—Five years are necessary to give the deaf a tolerable general understanding of their own language, so as to read, write,

write, and speak it, with ease.—The *manner* in which this is effected may in some measure be judged of, from what *hath been premised:*—namely, by first *shewing them* how the mouth is formed for production of the vowels, letting them *see* the external effect that vocalized breath hath upon the internal part of the wind-pipe, and causing them to *feel* with their thumbs and fingers the vibration of the larynx, first in the teacher, then in themselves.—When they found either of the vowels, then they are shewn the *written form* of what they have expressed, until they are perfected in the knowledge of the vowels or vocal sounds, to which succeeds the *formation* of syllables and words *as before described,* then the *meaning* of common words, and finally the *construction* of a *sentence* or sentences, out of which all descriptions of the mind or will are composed, or every exhibition

bition of *perception* or *volition*; which, as before observed, is the whole of language *.

In order also to effect this, they are at first taught the use of the letters or alphabetical characters, by names (or vocal forms) explanatory of their respective

* If then the leading powers of the soul be these two (perception and volition) it is plain that every speech or sentence, as far as it exhibits the soul, must of course respect one or other of these.—If we *assert*, then is it a sentence which respects the powers of *perception*, for what indeed is it to *assert* (if we consider the examples above alledged) but to *publish* some perception either of the senses, or the intellect?—Again, if we *interrogate*, if we *command*, if we *pray*, if we *wish* (which in terms of art is to speak sentences *interrogative, imperative, precative,* or *optative*) what do we but publish so many volitions?—For who is it that questions? He that *has a desire* to be informed—who is it that *commands?* He that *has a will*, which he would have obeyed.—*What are those beings* that either *wish* or *pray?* Those *who feel* certain *wants*, either for themselves or others. Harris's Hermes.

prac-

practical *powers,* such as *eb* for *B, ec* for *C, ed* for *D, fa* for *F, ga* for *G, oo* or *ou* for *W*, &c.

After this acquisition of the art of comprehending all the various combinations of the elements of speech, all wonder must cease at their attaining to perfection in other arts and sciences, *language* being the vehicle or instrument of communication;—and as the treatises on each art and science are (in these latter ages) become so common, when they are capable of understanding any publication, they are in possession of every requisite: nothing then but their own *application* is needful: that is encreased in *them* by a consciousness of its absolute necessity; for, as to sagacity, these pupils are *far enough* from any deficiency therein.

A mis-

A mistake or prejudice respecting the methods of teaching articulation, *I find* hath been imbibed by some, upon a supposition that harsh and severe methods were *privately used*, in order to enforce exertions contrary to their natural disposition and inclinations, and such a rigid discipline as is sometimes practised upon persons unfortutunately deprived of reason.—This error, I am bound by a regard to truth, (and also in justice to the worthy characters of these gentlemen) to confute: it is no less necessary, in order to obviate the discouraging effects of such an idea.—Nothing can possibly be more remote from a *true description of their methods*, for the most kind and affectionate mode is practised, much more tender, ingratiating, and consistent with the *true art of governing the human mind*, and making learning a pleasure, than *I ever* saw at any other school: the behaviour

viour of the pupils is the moſt convincing proof imaginable of this; they enter punctually the ſchool-room, with a degree of eagerneſs, they really love their learning, not regarding it (as young perſons in general do) as a hardſhip or impoſition, but as an *indulgence:* (the " drudgery" therefore mentioned by the author of the Origin and Progreſs of Language, is a mere figurative expreſſion as it relates to them, altho' it may be ſaid *literally* of the tutors, for they keep in no fixed ſeat in the ſchool, but are continually moving from one ſcholar to another.)

Such a remarkable affection and gratitude have theſe ſcholars to their teachers, that I knew an inſtance of a lady who was really apprehenſive of ſome *ſecret charm,* by which her child's affection would be more

more strongly fixed on Mr. Braidwood than on herself.

The only instrument made use of, except their own hands and the fingers of the instructor, is (I believe) a small round piece of silver, of a few inches long, the size of a tobacco-pipe, flatted at one end, with a ball (as large as a marble) at the other; by means of these the tongue is *gently* placed, at first, in the various positions respectively proper for forming the articulations of the different letters and syllables; until they acquire (as we all do, in learning speech) by *habit, the proper method*.

Those who know experimentally the tender concern of an *only* parent for an *only* son, even under the happiest circumstances of natural advantage, may imagine with what avidity the information of this Academy was first received: Altho' the authority was unquestionable, I, like many others, (I acknowledge) had doubts of the practicability of the business to any very *great degree*; I thought it my duty, however, to send my son across the Atlantic, upon Mr. Braidwood's agreeing to undertake the tuition of him, who accordingly received him in February, 1780.— He was then *eight years* old : although sprightly, sensible, and *quick of apprehension*, yet, having been either born *deaf*, or having lost his hearing by sickness in earliest infancy *, he could not *at that time* produce or distinguish *vocal* sounds, nor *articulate* at all, neither had he any idea of the meaning of words, either when

---

* His deafness was first (accidentally) discovered at the age of six months, when my solicitude commenced ; for I was then well apprized that the natural consequence must be want of speech, or language, unless a remedy for his deafness could be effected.

spoken,

spoken, in writing, or in print; and for *want of hearing*, would doubtless have remained as speechless as he was born.—I soon received the pleasing intelligence that he was beginning to articulate, and soon after that he could plainly express (upon seeing the form in characters) any word in the English language.

My first visit to him was in May, 1781. It exceeds the power of words to convey any idea of the sensations experienced at this interview.—The child, ambitious to manifest his acquisition, eagerly advanced, and addressed me, with a distinct salutation *of speech*. He also made several enquiries in *short* sentences.—I then delivered him a letter from his sister (couched in the *simplest* terms) which he read so as to be understood; he accompanied many of the words, *as he pronounced them*, with proper gestures,,

tures, fignificative of their meaning, fuch as in the fentence, "*write a letter by papa:*" on *uttering* the *firſt* word, he defcribed the action of writing, by the motion of his right-hand; the *ſecond*, by tapping the letter he held; the *third*, by pointing to me.—He could at that time repeat the Lord's Prayer very properly, and fome other forms, one of which in particular *(which I had never heard before)* I then took down in writing from his repetition; a convincing proof of his fpeaking intelligibly *.—I found he could in that fhort time read diftinctly, in *a ſlow manner*, any Englifh Book, although it cannot be fuppofed he had as yet learned *the meaning* of many words: he, however, made daily progrefs in that knowledge. As to writing, there can be no reafon why deaf

---

* The copy of the faid *ſhort* form, taken in writing, at the time, is in the Appendix.

perfons

persons may not, by imitation, learn that art as well as any other persons; accordingly I was not at all surprized, that he could write *very plainly:* this indeed he did with *uncommon readiness* and dexterity, and seemed not a little proud of all his new attainments.—I had also the satisfaction to see such specimens, at that time, *in the proficiency of others who had been longer* at this Academy, as left no doubt in my mind of his acquiring, in due season, a perfect acquaintance with *language* both oral and written; and that he would be capable of any art or science whatever, except *music and oratory.*—Perfectly satisfied with his situation, in a conscientious and respectable family, I left him to pursue his studies, with a degree of hope and joy, which, on this score, I had never expected to have known.—On my next visit, in September, 1782, his improvements were very perceptible in speech, the construction of language, and in writing: he had made a good beginning in *arithmetic,* and *surprizing* progress in the arts of drawing and *painting*.—I found him capable of not only comparing ideas, and drawing inferences, but expressing his sentiments with judgement.—On my desiring him to attempt something he thought himself unequal to, I set him the example by doing it myself: upon which, he shook his head, and, with a smile, replied (distinctly, *viva voce*) " *You are a man, Sir, I am a boy.*"— Observing, that he was inclined in company to converse with one of his schoolfellows, by the tacit finger-language, I asked him, why he did not speak to *him* with *his mouth*?—To this, his answer was as pertinent as it was concise, " *He is deaf.*" Many other instances I could mention of expressions of the mind, as proper as could be made by *any boy* of his age, who had *not* the disadvantage of deafness.

Several letters received from *Messrs. Braidwood*, (serving to inform of his improvements, as well as to shew their expectations of him) I found verified; of some of which the following are extracts, viz.

Edinburgh, 30 March, 1782.
" I have not the *smallest doubt*, but Mr.
" Charles will make a considerable figure
" in life, *notwithstanding his misfortune:*
" he is possessed of a strong genius, and
" gives very great application to every part
" of his learning.   T. B."

" *Edinburgh,* 20 *July,* 1782.
" We most heartily congratulate you on
" your son's improvements in drawing, and
         " in

"in *every other* branch of his *education:* if it fhould pleafe God to continue his health, he will *moſt undoubtedly* make a confiderable figure in life, which cannot fail to give you and every one concerned in him, great fatisfaction, to render him an *uſeful member of ſociety, happy* in himfelf, and an honour to us. You may depend, Sir, on our *utmoſt* attention to him in every refpect.

"As to the plan of his education (mentioned by you) we are of opinion, that he fhould be continued in the ftudy of the *Engliſh language, arithmetic, geography, geometry,* &c. until he is pretty much mafter of them. We think, if Charles is mafter of the Engliſh langnage, the *ſciences,* the *French,* and as much *Latin* as may give him a competent knowledge of the derivation of words, it
"would

" would be sufficient; and it would be a pity
" not to keep him employed as much as pos-
" sible in *drawing*, that appearing to be
" his *forte*.—As to dancing, we refer the
" time to yourself, &c.

" T. and J. Braidwood."

In short, I had the amplest opportunity of being convinced, that *those gentlemen do teach*, and have taught many, (who would otherwise have remained speechless and ignorant) so to exercise the voice and organs, as *in reality to speak, and converse intelligibly*, (viva voce) and, *in effect to hear*, as well as write and read grammatically, and of course made them capable (by their own application and assiduity) of attaining all the *useful* knowledge and learning of which the human mind is susceptible.—Several (of the many whom they have dismissed completely taught) are now employed

ployed in public offices, counting houses, and various branches of business. There was, the last time I was in Scotland, a gentleman at Leith, *(deaf, from his birth or early infancy)* who had been a pupil of Mr. Braidwood's. This gentleman has a thorough knowledge of the English language, and converses upon every subject very sensibly, (and as agreeably as a slow manner will admit); and I have seen many letters, written by others of his scholars, of both sexes, that, both with respect to grammatical composition, and sentiment, would do honour to any gentleman or lady.

The degree of *pronunciation*, of which they are capable, is proved by experience to be much greater than (until lately) was even thought *possible* by Mr. Braidwood himself; for *accent* and *emphasis*, strange as it may seem, are not unattainable by those

of

of them who are most docile, and have the happiest construction of organs, and good lungs; I have myself actually heard *one* of them repeat the Lord's Prayer, with a better accent and tone, than many clergymen do in the desk.

Thus one of the greatest misfortunes is reduced to little more than *a disadvantage in conversing*, and, in fact, in many respects inferior to many others.—It is to be lamented, that the social enjoyments of conversation are *too often* adulterated with a mixture unworthy of rational creatures. The improvement of the mind, and it's preparation for the more refined, intellectual enjoyments of a future state, is certainly the great end of this temporary, progressive existence; this preparation and improvement it appears to me, Mess. Braidwoods' deaf pupils are *hereby* made equally com-

competent to with others who hear.—
They may become *men of intellect and
science*, and capable of arriving at the
fummit and completion of human nature.
—What a contraft between the natural,
ufual ftate of perfons *born deaf*, and that
which (by this wonderful mode of inftruction and education) they are brought to!
—Their parents are only the inftruments
of Providence in giving them fenfitive and
animal exiftence: but as rational and converfible beings, capable of fpiritual as well
as temporal felicity, they may truly be faid
to be the offspring of thefe profeffors. And
if *Alexander* the Great thought himfelf
more indebted to *Ariftotle* who inftructed
him, than to *Philip* who gave him life and
empire, how much *more fo* thefe pupils to
men, from whom they receive the *moft incomparable and ineftimable* benefits!—Thefe
are not the lefs valuable becaufe not to be
realized

realized by a charm or miracle, that is, on a sudden; or by a few leſſons: it *muſt* be the work of time, and unremitted perſeverance, for years, under the conſtant eye of the teacher, who gives "*line upon line, and precept upon precept, here a little, and there a little;*" not only in ſchool, but at meals, in walking, playing, &c. and upon all occaſions making a leſſon out of every ſuitable occurrence:— but what *time* or *expence* can be *too much* to beſtow for acquiſitions of ſuch *infinite* conſequence to the individual?

The effect of this inſtruction is, alſo, that inſtead of being the moſt "dull and ſolitary" of all human beings, they become remarkable *chearful* and ſocial.

Every thing that is new and very extraordinary is apt to ſtrike with a degree of aſtoniſh-

astonishment that lessens its own credibility: the opinion I am now going to hazard will therefore, doubtless, be esteemed romantic, or the effect of an heated imagination: nevertheless, from what I have seen, it is my serious persuasion, that the operation of the mind, *in deaf* persons *(thus instructed,)* not being so liable to be *diverted* or disturbed, (by the noises or sounds that frequently occur,) as *in others*, their application to any point in science may be more uniformly intense, and consequently their *powers of abstraction greater than ordinary*; and I have no doubt but that some of them, who are possessed of genius, will make mathematical discoveries of great importance, and carry their researches in philosophy beyond those of other men: And thus the ways of Providence which, in many respects, are inscrutable, and past finding

finding out, may, in a new instance, be justified to man *.

When the art of *reading* was first in use, which is now so common and extensively useful, it was *wonderful* to the vulgar, and considered as preternatural.

How invaluable, however, are the blessings, temporal and eternal, which *they* may *derive* to *themselves*, from the power of cultivating their own minds! It was a saying of one of the antient heathen philosophers (dictated by the light of nature) that, " *The man who could live* in the " pure enjoyment of his *mind*, and who " properly *cultivated* that divine principle,

---

* " And thus for the honour of *culture*, and good
" learning, they are able to render a *man* (if he will
" take the pains) *intrinsically more excellent* than his
" *naturally superior.*"

Harris's Hermes.

" was

" was *happiest* in himself, and most beloved
" *by the gods, for that the gods* rejoiced in
" what was *most essentially excellent*, and by
" nature the nearest allied to themselves,
" viz. *mind* *."

Besides teaching the *deaf*, there is another art, of vast (although of less) importance, taught at this Academy, which many have experienced the good effect of, viz. *removing impediments in speech.*

" The grosser faults of articulation" (says Mr. *Sheridan* on Elocution) " such as stut-
" tering, hesitation, lisping, and inability
" to pronounce certain letters, can never

---

* " All *minds* that are, are similiar and congenial,
" and so too are their *ideas*, or intelligible forms;
" were it otherwise, there could be no intercourse be-
" tween *man* and *man*, or *what is more important*, be-
" tween *man* and *God*."

Harris's Hermes.

" be

"be cured by *precept alone.* These re-
"quire the constant aid of a person skilled in
"the causes of those faults, who, by teach-
"ing each individual, *how to use the organs
"of speech rightly,* and by shewing him the
"proper position of the tongue, lips, &c.
"*may gradually* bring him to a just articu-
"lation."

I knew two young gentlemen, sons of a merchant of Greenock, who were entirely cured of this defect; one of them, his father assured me, before he went to Mr. Braidwood, was troubled with such a violent stammering, that it was very painful to be witness to it, who, when I saw him in June, 1781, could repeat the most difficult soliloquy, with perfect ease and *gracefulness,* and would converse the whole day, without once discovering any remains of his former impediment.

It is much to be regretted, that since the time Messrs. Braidwood began to practice this ingenious method, these gentlemen have been under the mortifying and cruel necessity of refusing the charge and instruction, as I understand, of upwards of *an hundred* (chiefly *deaf* persons). Although they have with *humanity, benevolence,* and *generosity,* maintained and taught several children of indigent parents *gratis,* yet that violence have they been obliged to do to their inclinations, for the following good reasons : First, it would have been eventually deceiving themselves, as well as their pupils and their friends ; *labouring without thorough effect,* consequently bringing into contempt and disuse a method, which with no small labor and assiduity they have brought to a great degree of perfection, were they *(themselves)* to pretend to instruct more than a certain number at a time ;

time; their joint attention and tuition cannot (I think) be applied to many more than *twenty*, at once, with full effect.

Secondly, a necessary and laudable regard to their own family forbade their undertaking what must be an insupportable burthen to any single family; for many of the parents of such objects were incapable even of reimbursing the necessary expences of maintenance, &c.—It is greatly desireable, that this difficulty may be removed by adopting the subjoined * or a similar plan.

And here, I am happy to avail myself of an opportunity of bearing my *public* testimony to the *merits* of these gentlemen, both as professors and as men: Gratitude, I think, demands it; for no *pecuniary* com-

* Vide Appendix.

penfation can ever, in my opinion, dif-charge the obligation which every *affectionate parent* of any *fenfibility* muſt *feel*: the weight of which equally furpaſſes the ability of my pen to make adequate acknowledgement of.—As, however, Meſſrs. Braidwood's reputation *neither needs the tribute* of my applauſe, nor *can receive* any advantage from the encomiums of an *individual in private* life, ſo I ſhould wiſh to avoid offending delicacy, by any expreſ-ſions that might be conſtrued into adula-lation.—It is for the ſake of *many particular members* in every fociety, that I have taken up the quill on this occaſion:—But, *If,* " HE *that makes* TWO *blades of grafs grow* " *where only one grew before, hath more merit* " *than the whole race of politicians,"* what SUPERIOR CREDIT *and diſtinguiſhing* HONORS are due to the *fuccefsful cultivator of thoſe grounds of human reafon, which would*

other-

otherwise have been an UNPRODUCTIVE, BARREN, *and* DREARY WILDERNESS!

N.B. Mr. Braidwood hath frequently intimated to me, as an opinion founded upon his experience in this art, that *articulate* or spoken language hath so great and essential a tendency to confirm and enlarge ideas, above the power of *written* language, that it is almost impossible for *deaf* persons, without the use of *speech*, to be *perfect* in their ideas.

He, however, doubts whether there is any such thing as a real, natural " non compos mentis;" and supposes *ideotcy* to be always the effect of a *disordered* or *extremely weak* and relaxed constitution of body.—He hath related to me several instances of young persons in a very weak state of body, who were *supposed ideots*, whom, by a proper attention to the physical causes, (and by astringent medicines, together with the Cold-Bath, and other suitable means), he hath brought, first, to a greater degree of strength, and afterwards to exert their rational faculties:—certain it is, that the connexion between the mind and body is such, that they interchangeably, in all cases, partake of the state of each other; which may, *perhaps*, justify that gentleman's opinion, that there are none of the human race, in whom the mind (of itself) is absolutely incapable, *by nature*, of *any* improvement.

PART III.

PROPOSAL

TO

Perpetuate and extend the Benefits of this important Art.

FROM a consideration of the case of the naturally-deaf, their capacity of becoming happy in themselves, and useful in society, in consequence of this admirable method of qualification; and, from their *numbers, (which greatly exceed what is generally known)* of the impossibility of these gentlemen, alone, receiving and teaching all who have applied, and who stand in need of tuition; from these considerations (I say) many of the first and most respectable characters within these realms,

realms, have manifested an humane and truly benevolent disposition to establish a *public, charitable institution*, for the certain continuance and extention of the benefits of this important art, more particularly, as a blessing to the children of *indigent parents*.

To promote so worthy a design, and to enforce its expediency, must surely need but little argument.

The present professors of this art, like all other men, " whose breath is in their " nostrils," may be suddenly taken away, before any successors are duly qualified.

The humiliating and pitiable *state* of such as *remain both deaf and dumb*, cannot need any further description.—As to their *capacities*, as it hath been demonstrated,
" that

that they are vested with *all the powers of the soul*, they are, by inevitable inference, capable, when instructed, not only of *knowing*, but of *obeying the laws both of God and man*: The means, only, of the publication of *those powers* (of perception and volition) which the generality of the human race are blessed with, namely *speech*, they have *not indeed* the usual facility of acquiring; but it is, I hope, ere now credible, that, with *greater perseverance*, and the use of the ingenious modes already spoken of herein, they are *capable of acquiring* the *happy faculty (of speech,)* although not fluency.

The *numbers* born in every generation, and in every country, under this disadvantage, or in whom this " Lapsus Naturæ" (of deafness) is exhibited, (and who have been in former ages lost to the world), are
not

not a few: there are inftances of fix or feven in one family only, and it is computed, that feveral hundred of various ages are, *at this day,* exifting in this ifland alone.

It would be difficult for me to afcertain exactly the number *at prefent* in this predicament : *Dr. Bulwer* mentions a vaft many inftances, *in his day* *, in Europe, and feveral of *whole families,* and then proceeds as follows,

" Nor are examples of thefe fad acci-
" dents very rare among *us* ; fuch therfore
" as I have either knowne, or by credible
" intelligence gained notice of from others,
" I fhall here annex ; conceiving it fit to
" enlarge the foreigne ftory of *deafe* and
" *dumbe* men, with fuch additional notions.
" The rather that *wee* may come a little out

* 1648.

" of thefe outlandifh writers debt, and in
" fome reafonable fort vie hiftoricall obfer-
" vations with them.

" *Sir Edward Goſtwicke* of *Wellington* in
" the county of Bedfordſhire, baronet, a
" gentleman otherwife very accompliſhed,
" was borne *deafe* and *dumbe*; he hath at-
" tained unto writing, which is a fubfti-
" tute of fpeech, and from whence there
" lies a way, if well followed, to the re-
" covery of articulate voyce. Hence,
" writing, to them that are *deafe* and *dumbe*
" may ferve inftead of fpeech, who there-
" fore doe beft *begin* to write, and *after-*
" *wards* to fpeake. The firft invention of
" writing was to make *verba viſibilia, miſ-*
" *ſilia, & permanentia*, to remedy the defect
" of fpeech that vaniſheth away, is onely
" audible, and cannot bee wrought into
" difcourfe but by two that are prefent to-
" gether,

"gether, whereas this invention puts an
"eare, as it were, into the eye, and pre-
"fents our cogitations vifible and legible,
"writing being the later invention: Speech
"by itfelfe fignifies all our conceptions,
"and writing fignifies our fpeech, for
"writing is to words, as words to cogita
"tions. Yet this order is not of neceffity,
"fo that the contrary cannot bee done:
"but it happens rather by reafon of the
"facility, and becaufe men that are de-
"prived of none of their fenfes are apt
"fooner to fpeake than to write, the tongue
"being fooner fitted by nature for that
"employment than the hand for this, but
"the cleane contrarie may be done, as ap-
"pears in the atchievement of this *honor-*
"*able* gentleman and others mentioned in
"this book, &c."

"The

"The *youngest brother* of the said Sir
"*Edward Goftwicke* is in the same condi-
"tion, being yet an eminent limbner, in-
"vited to that art by his genius, or some
"signalitie of spirit observed in him,
"*painting* and *limbning*, next to writing,
"having ever been thought of excellent
"use, and to afford singular contentation,
"to those that are borne deafe and dumbe.
"And therefore *Q. Pedius* (the nephew of
"O. Pedius, a man of consular dignity,
"and one that had triumphed, by *Cæsar*
"dictator made co-heir with *Anguftus*)
"being *dumbe* by nature, Meſſala, the ora-
"tour of whose familie the grandmother
"of the childe was descended, being care-
"ful how the boy should be brought up,
"after mature advise and deliberation,
"thought good that he should by signes
"and imitation be trained in the art of
"painting; and Auguftus Cæfar approved
"of

" of his judgement and advice herein: and
" in truth, the young gentleman being apt
" thereto, (although he died a youth)
" was growne a great proficient in that art.

" *Sir John Keyes*, master of the ordi-
" nance to King James, had *two* sisters,
" who were both born *deafe* and dumbe:
" they could *write*, and were very inge-
" genious to imitate any kind of needle-
" work they saw.

" *Sir Miles Fleetwood* had *two* hand-
" some gentlewomen to his daughters, both
" borne *deafe* and *dumbe*.

" *De la Barre*, the rich Dutch mer-
" chant who lived at Eeling in Middlesex,
" had *two* daughters borne *deafe and*
" *dumbe*; they were both married; a
" friend of mine, who was in their com-
panies

" panies at Brainford, their hufbands alfo
" being there) told me he did much ad-
" mire at their dexterity of perception;
" for by the leaft motion of their hufbands
" countenance or hand, they prefently
" conceived of the meaning.

" Mafter *Freeman*, of London, fkin-
" ner, had *two* daughters, both *deafe* and
" *dumbe*.

" One mafter *Diet*, a parfon in Staf-
" fordfhire, had a brother and fifter,
" both *deafe* and dumbe.

" One *Thomas King*, farmer of Lang-
" ley, in the county of Effex, had by
" one woman a *fon* and *three* daughters,
" *all* deafe and dumbe.

" One

" One in *Ofmafton*, within a mile of
" Derby, had foure fonnes, and all of
" them born deafe and dumbe.

" One *John Gardiner*, of Thaxted in
" Effex, had a *fonne* and *daughter*, both
" *deafe* and dumbe : his fon, Robert Gar-
" diner, is a tradefman here in town, and
" one of the moft notable examples I have
" difcovered, for proofe of the feeling of
" founds : and whom, to the fatisfaction
" and admiration of fome freinds of mine,
" I have fhewed and expofed to a philofo-
" phicall view and tryall.

" And, as I am informed by a merchant of
" credit living in London, there was in Lin-
" colnfhire, one mafter *Dallifon*, a gentle-
" man that ufed grazing, who had three
" fonnes borne deafe and dumbe, who
" made them all three graziers, and they
" proved

" proved the craftiest in that way the
' country ever bred, &c.

" One master *Adams*, in the east of
" Kent, had two daughters, very hand-
" some, proper gentlewomen, which were
" *all the children* he had, and they were
" both *deafe* and *dumb*.

" A husbandman of Sherrington, with-
" in a mile of Newport (Buckingham-
" shire), had a *sonne* and daughter, both
" deafe and dumb.

" A husbandman of Tilstone (in Che-
" shire) about seven miles from Chester,
" had two daughters, twins, that were both
" *deafe* and *dumbe*," &c.

Bulwar's Philoc. pp. 81—87.

In all thirty-one within his own knowledge.

Is it not an object worthy of every *expanded* heart, to provide certain and important relief to so many fellow-partakers of human nature, and in its effects to all their respective connexions?

To render this art universally useful, it is necessary that some ingenious young men should be instructed and qualified to assist, and succeed the present professors, and that a fund should be established under the direction of proper managers, to be applied to the purpose of educating those whose parents are altogether unable to defray such expence, and to assist others who can afford a part but not the whole, by which means, *all* the deaf, however scattered, might be collected, and taught, and consequently rescued from certain ignorance, from idleness, and from want, as well as
every

every defect in speech (however inconvenient and violent) rectified.

Messrs. Braidwood have repeatedly declared their readiness to undertake to qualify a sufficient number of young men for the execution of such a plan.

In an age distinguished by so many public charities, and ready to encourage every *useful* invention in arts and sciences, more especially in *these kingdoms*, which so remarkably abounds with generous and noble institutions for the relief of *almost* every species of misery; where provision is made for the prevention, or remedy, of such variety of evils, natural and moral; (and indeed *in every civilized country*) the feelings of human nature cannot fail to be roused, in favour of a *well-directed* scheme, of this nature; not can it be doubted but that a fund for this purpofe might *eafily* be raifed.

A fund *fairly* fet on foot, the proper and *judicious* application of it *clearly afcertained, muft*, doubtlefs meet with ample encouragement from the *very many* well-difpofed, and opulent, whofe contributions, I am convinced, would be ready for a defign of fo *humane* and *beneficial* a nature. Under the direction of a refpectable governor and directors for the management of the fund, there is every reafon to hope and believe, that, upon a proper application to THEIR MAJESTIES, it would originate in the bounty and patronage of the crown.

In addition to the other acts of royal munificence which reflect peculiar dignity on both thofe illuftrious and amiable characters,

racters, this new proof of their tenderneſs towards every object of *charitable* attention, *we may be certain*, would not be withheld.—If by their gracious approbation and countenance, they ſhould be principally inſtrumental in the hands of Providence, in tranſmitting to poſterity the benefits of this *uſeful* and extraordinary invention, *which hath been perfected in their reign* (a bleſſing unknown in former ages); many, not only in this, but in generations yet unborn, may by a new and *ſingular mode*, yield their teſtimony to ſuch *exalted* merit; and even *(otherwiſe) mute* tongues and voices *articulate* a grateful tribute of acknowledgement to their great and *royal benefactors.* The forcible and extenſive influence of their virtuous examples would, doubtleſs, (as it often hath) be very ſenſibly perceptible in this inſtance*.

Sub-

---

* I have lately been made acquainted with his Majeſty's having been graciouſly pleaſed conditionally to give

Subscriptions opened under the direction of the authority of the governor and directors, upon a plan similar (or perhaps preferable) to that of which a sketch is hereto *subjoined*, mentioning that the contributions of the public, and the sole distribution of the fund is vested in the said governor and directors, and that those who wish their connexions to partake of the benefits of this institution, must apply to them, would probably be encouraged: by this means, the interest might be forever secured from becoming a sinecure, and certain provisions made for the continuance of the art.

Some perhaps, whose hearts are exempt from an *inconvenient* degree of sensibility, may possibly object, that the utility hereof,

---

give 100*l.* per annum, out of his private purse, for this purpose.

to

to thofe born of *poor* parents, is not *very great*, and as their ferviceablenefs would not be *much enlarged* in the lower fpheres of life, fo on their account it would be of *but little advantage.*—I deny both premifes and inference.—Firft, their ufefulnefs is exceedingly encreafed, even for the loweft ftations, and particularly as domeftics, of which I have had feveral occafions to be convinced. Indeed no further argument in proof can be neceffary, than this, which every one muft allow, i. e. the perfon who *knows* what is faid, and can reply *intelligibly*, is certainly vaftly more capable of receiving and executing commands than he who cannot do either. And as to his welfare, to alledge, that it is not of much importance on that fcore, is to fay, that for a rational creature to be made acquainted with his duty and intereft as a member of fociety, the end and defign of his being, &c. is a matter of no confequence to to him. But, *if the soul is immortal*, is not a *poor* man's soul as much " *more valuable than the whole world,*" as the soul of any Dives? Is it not an emanation from the *same* Author of Being, who is no respecter of persons?—Or are any so thoughtless as to suppose, that the " vital spark of heavenly flame" is not alive in naturally *deaf* persons!—But, upon a supposition *(the most execrable, as well as erroneous, imaginable)* that the *poor* are not worthy of happiness *here,* or hereafter, is there any station so exalted, or fortune so affluent, as to ensure a parent or a family from the beforementioned circumstance of the organs of hearing in a child, or near connexion, being deranged in fœtu, or before birth, as is generally the case with such persons?—Then, let it be again observed, that *one great* end of this proposed institution is, to transmit to the end of time, for the benefit of *every class,*

class, this infinitely beneficial method of communication.—I know no other probable objections, except such superstitious ones, as formerly prevailed against *another remedy* for a terrible calamity, which Providence most mercifully favoured the world with—I mean, *inoculation* for the smallpox.

To those, in either case, the same answer is pertinent, viz. that every means which Providence points out, as alleviations of natural evil, it is the duty of men to embrace with gratitude.

It is universally considered (except among savages) as *naturally incumbent* on parents in general, while they teach their children *to speak*, to make them *sensible of their duty* in every relation, of the source *from whence life* and understanding flows, of the chief end and design

design of our existence here; and to instil into their minds *the hope* and expectation of a *future state*; this, all conscientious parents, in a state of civilization, observe; many are indefatigable in inculcating these parts of knowledge; justly thinking no pains too great, by which they be ingrafted in their youthful minds:—Some capacities (it was observed at first) require more cultivation than others; those therefore, whose offspring, from *peculiar circumstances*, require much more attention to complete them, as "*beings of the next order to angels*," have received a greater charge, and more will be required, in proportion to their abilities, at their hands. But many are incapable of effectuating their good wishes for their children born under these disadvantages; it therefore becomes, in a manner, the *duty of communities*, in those cases, to lend their combined aid to such parents,

parents, by enabling them to improve the extraordinary means Providence hath kindly afforded.

The Lacedemonians, of old, regarded children as the property of society, and wisely considered it not only justifiable, but expedient, and incumbent, to make the *instruction* and *qualification* of the rising generation the care of the public, and of course obliged parents to deliver them into the hands appointed therefor:—If then, such as seemed to require no other advantages, or assistance, than such as parents *(in these days)* take upon themselves to give, were deemed bound to be qualified *by society*, for *usefulness* here, and happiness hereafter, how much *more* must it appear *commendable* to take such children out of those parents hands, who not only appear incapable of doing more for them than sustaining animal existence, but whose hearts

hearts must be rejoiced beyond measure at the event!

Sensible how much the love of fashionable pleasure and dissipation prevail over the sublime and refined speculations of philosophy and religion, I am well aware that a comparatively great number of mankind will turn away with disgust from a scheme, in which there is so little to contribute to their *own amusement*, and that a plan for erecting a new house for an *exotic* singer or dancer, would interest *the bulk* of mankind more than any design for the improvement of the mind; notwithstanding which, there are, doubtless, *enough* in this and every nation *of a more elevated*, and extensive turn.—*The Royal Society* have heretofore given encouragement to the progagation of the *theory* of this art, and would doubtless countenance the establishment of *its practice*.

The *learned, pious,* and *opulent* body of dignified *clergymen,* as well as numbers of *that character* among all ranks of the laity, would certainly rejoice in promoting the means of making *every soul* acquainted with the Revealed Will of God, as well as capacitating them for social *communication,* the means of self-enjoyment no less than of utility to society. That elegant writer *St. Paul* asks, with respect to the means of *salvation* in general, " how shall they *hear* without a *preacher?*" which, with due deference, may, in this instance, be paraphrased, *How* shall they (the naturally deaf) *learn* without *a teacher?*

The satisfaction of *all* good men must surely be in proportion to their opportunities of beneficence. The reflexion that *not* the immediate objects *only* (of this plan), but the respective circles of their connexions,
must

must be greatly benefited, and made much happier, cannot but augment the satisfaction. As the pebble thrown into the calm, stagnant lake, first forms a small single ring, and thence extending takes in the whole surface, within its influence, so will the contributions to this scheme so worthy of humanity, first be felt with *peculiar* force, and in its effects comprehend the felicity of *many circles.*

By the accomplishment of some such plan (which will be executed if a favourable disposition in the public is not wanting) one less evil will henceforth be found in society: For, amongst those who are not deficient in understanding, there, *never more,* need be *any dumb person.* No expressions occur to me so adequate to my own ideas, as those used by the *noblest,* moral,

English poet*, on *the principle of universal benevolence*, with which I will close my reflexions on this subject.

" In *faith* and *hope*, the world *will disagree*,
" But *all* mankind's concern is CHARITY;
" All MUST be *false* that thwart *this one*
 " great end;
" And *all* of GOD, that BLESS mankind,
 " or MEND."

* Pope.

APPENDIX.

Extracts from various Authors, on the Subject of Messrs. *Braidwoods'* Academy.

1st,—Extract from *Arnot's* History of Edinburgh.

" Of the Academy of *Deaf and Dumb*."

" BESIDES the schools and colleges of public institution, a school of the *most curious* and *important* nature is taught by *Mr. Braidwood*, for it may be said *in effect* to give the *deaf* to hear, the *dumb* to speak.—Mr. Braidwood
" first

"first attempted this art about the year
" 1764 *. He began with a single pupil;
" he has now a number of pupils, mostly
" from England, but some also from Ame-
" rica: and his success in teaching them
" has exceeded his own expectations. He
" begins with learning the deaf, articula-
" tion, or the use of their vocal organs,
" and at the same time teaches them to
" write the characters, and compose
" *words* of them. He next shews them
" the use of words in expressing *visible ob-*
" *jects* and their *qualities:* after this, he
" proceeds to instruct them in the proper
" *arrangement* of words, or grammatical
" *construction* of language. The *deaf* (Mr.
" Braidwood observes) find great difficulty
" in attaining pronunciation, but still more in
" acquiring a proper knowledge of written

* This is an error of the author or printer.— It ws in 1760.

" language.

"language.—Their only method of con-
"versing (*naturally* *) is by signs and ges-
"tures: their ideas being few are (*pre-
"vious to his instructions* *) confined to
"visible objects, and to the passions or
"senses; the former of which they delineate
"by figures, the latter by gestures:—The
"connexion between our ideas and written
"language being purely arbitrary, it is a
"very hard task to give the deaf any no-
"tion of that mode of conversing, theirs
"being only hieroglyphical; another still
"greater difficulty is to enable them to
"comprehend the meaning of the figura-
"tive part of language: for instance, they
"soon understand *high, low, hard, tender,
"clear, cloudy, &c.* when applied to *mat-
"ter,* but have not the smallest concep-

* Those words in parentheses in this page are not in the original, but were doubtless meant to be *understood*, by the author.

"tion

" tion of these qualities, when applied to
" the *mind*.—Notwithstanding these diffi-
" culties, the deaf attain a perfect know-
" ledge of written language, and become
" capable both of speaking and writing
" their sentiments in the most distinct man-
" ner, and of understanding what they read:
" being thus advanced, they are capable
" to learn any art or science (music ex-
" cepted), and to translate one language
" into another;—Mr. Braidwood's pupils
" are under his tuition from three to six
" years, according to their age, capacity,
" and conveniency.—When we visited this
" Academy, we found that the boys could
" not only converse by the help of the
" artificial alphabet they learnt, by put-
" ting their fingers into certain positions,
" but that they understood us, altho' per-
" fect strangers to them, by the motions
" of our lips. In this manner, they ac-
                                    " tually

"tually conversed with us, returning
"an anſwer diſtinctly, yet ſlowly, *viva*
"*voce.*—It is needleſs to expatiate upon
"*the encouragement due to the author of a*
"*mode of inſtruction ſo ingenious, as well as*
"*important* to an unfortunate part of man-
"kind. We cannot conclude without ex-
"preſſing our hopes, that this valuable art
"does not depend upon the precarious te-
"nure of a ſingle life; but that Mr. *Braid-*
"*wood* has communicated ſo much of his
"method as to enable ſome one to give
"ſimilar inſtruction."

Arnot's Hiſt. of Edin. p. 425.

2dly, Extract from Dr. *Johnſon's* Journey to the Weſtern Iſlands of Scotland.

"There is one ſubject of philoſophical
"curioſity to be found in *Edinburgh*,
"which

" which no other city has to shew; a col-
" lege of the *deaf* and dumb, who are
" taught to *speak*, to *read*, to *write*, and
" to practise *arithmetic*, by a gentleman
" whose name is !*Braidwood:* the number
" which attends him is, *I think*, about
" twelve; which he brings together into a
" little school, and instructs according to
" their several degrees of proficiency:—I
" do not mean to mention the instruction of
" the deaf as *new:* — having been first
" practised upon the son of a constable of
" Spain, it was afterwards cultivated with
" much emulation in England by *Wallis*
" and *Holder*; and was lately professed by
" Mr. *Baker*, who once flattered me with
" hopes of seeing his method published.
" —How far any *former teachers* have suc-
" ceeded, it is not easy to know.

" The

"The improvement of *Mr. Braidwood's* *pupils is wonderful:* they not only *speak, write,* and underſtand what is written, but if he that ſpeaks looks towards them, and modifies his organs by diſtinct and full utterance, they know ſo well what is ſpoken, that it is an expreſſion *ſcarcely figurative* to ſay, *They hear with the eye.*—That any have attained to the power mentioned by Burnet, of feeling ſounds by laying a hand on the ſpeaker's mouth, I know not; but I have ſeen ſo much that I can believe more; a *ſingle word,* or a ſhort ſentence, I think, *may* poſſibly, be ſo diſtinguiſhed.— It will readily be ſuppoſed by thoſe that conſider this ſubject, that Mr. Braidwood's ſcholars ſpell accurately: orthography is vitiated among ſuch as *learn firſt* to ſpeak, and then to write, by imperfect notions of the relations between letters and

"and vocal utterance; but to those stu-
"dents every character is of equal impor-
"tance; for letters are to them *not* sym-
"bols of names, but of things; when
"they write they do not represent a *sound*,
"but delineate a *form* :—this school I vi-
"sited, and found some of the scholars
"waiting for their master, whom they are
"said to receive at his entrance with smil-
"ing countenances and sparkling eyes, *de-*
"*lighted* with the hope of new ideas.—
"One of the young ladies had her slate
"before her, on which I wrote a question
"consisting of three figures to be multi-
"plied by two figures. She looked upon
"it, and quivering her fingers in a manner
"which I thought very pretty, but of
"which I know not whether it was art or
"play, multiplied the sum regularly in two
"lines, observing the decimal place; but
"did not add the two lines together, pro-
"bably

"bably *disdaining so easy an operation:* I
"pointed at the place where the sum total
"should stand, and she noted it with *such
"expedition* as seemed to shew, she had it
"only to write:—It was pleasing to see
"one of the most *desperate of human ca-
"lamities* capable of so much help.—
"Whatever enlarges hope will exalt cou-
"rage. After seeing the deaf taught arith-
"metic, who would be afraid to cultivate
"the Hebrides?"

> Johnson's Journey to the Western Islands
> of Scotland.

3dly, Extract from "The Origin and Progress of Language" (by Lord Monboddo)
published 1773.

"ARGUMENT.
"That articulation is *not natural* to man."

"But

"But what puts the matter out of all doubt, in my apprehension, is the case of *deaf persons* among us; and their case deserves to be more attentively considered, that they are precisely in the condition, in which we suppose men to have been in the natural state: for, *like them*, they have the organs of pronunciation, and, like them too, they have *inarticulate cries*, by which they express their wants and desires: they have likewise, by constant intercourse with men who have the use of reason, and who converse with them *in their way*, acquired the habit of forming ideas (which we must suppose the savage to have acquired, tho' with infinitely more labor, before he could have a language to express them)."—"They *(the naturally* [*]

---

[*] Understood.

deaf)

" *deaf*) want therefore nothing in order to
" *speak* but *inſtruction* or example, which
" ſavages, who invented the firſt language,
" likewiſe wanted :—In this ſituation, do
" *they* invent a language, when they come
" to perfect age? (as it is ſuppoſed we all
" ſhould do, if we had not learned one in
" our infancy).—Or do *they* ever come to
" ſpeak during their whole lives? The
" fact moſt certainly is, *they never do*, but
" communicate their thoughts by looks
" and geſtures, which we call ſigns, **unleſs**
" *they be taught to articulate by an art lately*
" *invented*." Vol. I. p. 177, 8.

" I knew two profeſſors of the art in
" Paris; one of them Monſ. *l'Abbé de*
" *l'Epée*, with whom I was ſeveral times,
" and whoſe civility, and the trouble he
" took to ſhew his method of teaching, I
" take this opportunity of acknowledging:
" he

"he had brought *one* of his scholars a surprizing length, and one of them I particularly remember, who spoke so pleasantly, that I should not have known her to be *deaf*.—There is at present at Edinburgh a professor of the same art, *Mr. Braidwood*, whom I know, and who has likewise been at the trouble of shewing me *his method of teaching*, which I very much approve.—He has taught *many*, with great success, and there is one of his scholars, particularly, who is presently * carrying on the business of a painter in London, and who both *speaks* and *writes* good English.—But it is surprizing what labor it costs *him to teach*, and his scholars to learn, which puts it out of all doubt that articulation is not only an art, but an art of most difficult

* 1773.

" acquisition, otherwise than by *imitation*
" *and constant practice* from our earliest
" years: for, in the first place, it is diffi-
" cult to teach those scholars to make any
" sound at all; they at first only breathe
" strongly, till they are taught to make
" that concussion and tremulous motion of
" the wind-pipe, which produces audible
" sounds; these are very *harsh, low*, and
" guttural, *at first*, and more like croak-
" ing than a clear vocal sound." P. 179.

—" After this difficulty, which is not
" small, is got over, then comes the
" chief labor, to teach them the pronun-
" ciation of the several letters; in doing
" which, the teacher is obliged, not only
" himself to use many distortions and gri-
" maces, in order to shew his scholars the
" position and action of the several organs;
" but likewise to employ his hands to
" place

"place and move their organs, properly;
"while the scholars themselves labor
"so much, and bestow such pains and
"attention, that I am really surprized,
"that *with all the desire they have to
"learn*, which is very great, they should
"be able to support the drudgery; and
"I am assured by Mr. *Braidwood*, that
"if he did not take *different* methods
"with them, according to their different
"capacities, and the difference of their
"organs, it *would be impossible* to teach
"many of them." P. 181.

"If therefore this art be so difficult to
"be learnt without imitation, even by the
"assistance of the most diligent instruction,
"how much more difficult must the inven-
"tion of it have been; that is, the acqui-
"sition of it without either instruction or
"example!

"Having

"Having thus proved the fact (as I
"think) inconteſtibly, it will not be diffi-
"cult to aſſign the reaſons, and explain
"the theory; for we need only conſider
"with a little attention the *mechaniſm* of
"ſpeech, and we ſhall ſoon find, that there
"is required for ſpeaking, *certain poſitions*
"and *motions* of the organs of the mouth;
"ſuch as, the tongue, the teeth, lips, and
"palate, that cannot be from nature, but
"muſt be the effect of art; for their
"action, when they are employed in the
"enunciation of ſpeech, is ſo different from
"their natural and quieſcent ſituation, that
"nothing but long uſe and exerciſe could
"have taught us to employ them in that
"way.

"To explain this more particularly is
"*not neceſſary* for my preſent purpoſe; I
"ſhall have occaſion to treat of it after-
"wards;

P

"wards; but, who would defire, in the
"mean time, to be better informed about
"it, may confult *Dionyfius* the Halicarnaf-
"fian, in his Treatife of Compofition,
"where he has moft accurately explained
"the different operations of the organs in
"the pronunciation of the different letters;
"and whoever would defire *to be ftill far-*
"*ther informed, let him attend Mr. Braid-*
"*wood when he teaches, who, from his*
"*practice in that way, has learned to know*
"*more of the mechanifm of language, than*
"*any* grammarian or philofopher.—I fhall
"only fay further on this fubject, that
"pronunciation is one of thofe arts of
"which the inftruments are the members
"of the human body, like *dancing,* and
"another art more akin to this: I mean,
"*finging*; and, like thofe arts, *it is learnt*
"*either by mere imitation* (man, being as
"as Ariftotle has told us, the moft imitative
"of

" of all animals); or *by teaching,* as in the case of deaf persons, but joined with very constant and assiduous practice, that being absolutely necessary for the acquiring of *any art, in whichever of the two ways it is learnt.*"

" And here we may observe, that it is a very false conclusion, to infer from the facility of doing any thing, that it is a *natural operation:* for what is it that we do more easily or readily than speaking? —And yet we see, it is *an art,* that is *not to be taught without* the greatest labor and difficulty, both on the part of the master and the scholar: *nor to be learned by imitation without continual practice,* from our infancy upwards: for *it is not* to be learned like other arts, such as dancing and singing, by practising an hour or *two a day, for a few years,* or " perhaps

"perhaps only some months; but constant
"and *uninterrupted* practice is required *for*
"*many years*, and for *every hour*, I may
"say, *every minute* of the day *."

Monboddo on the Orig. and Prog. of Lang. Vol. I. pp. 182, 183, 184.

4thly, — Extract from Mr. *Pennant's* Tour through Scotland, in 1772.

"On returning into the city, I called at
"*Mr. Braidwood's Academy* of *Deaf* and
"*Dumb.* — This extraordinary professor
"had under his care a number of young

---

* As Lord Monboddo's Treatise is a chain of arguments, and as other proofs in support thereof are interwoven with the above extracts, I have taken the liberty to adduce from the mixture such parts only as immediately relate to the point in hand, viz. of giving speech to *naturally* or *eventually* deaf persons, and such as are essential to the proposed purpose of this publication.

"per-

" perfons, who had received the *Prome-*
" *thean* heat, the *divine* inflatus, but from
" the unhappy conftruction of their organs
" were (until they received his inftruc-
" tion) denied the power of utterance:—
" every idea was locked up, or appeared
" but in their eyes, or at their fingers
" ends, till their mafter inftructed them in
" arts unknown to us, who have the fa-
" culty of hearing.—Apprehenfion reaches
" *us* by the groffer fenfes;—*they* fee our
" words, and our uttered thoughts become
" to them vifible: our ideas expreffed in
" fpeech ftrike *their ears* in vain; *their
" eyes* receive them as they part from our lips;
" they conceive by intuition, and fpeak by
" imitation.—Mr. Braidwood firft teaches
" them the letters and their powers, and
" the ideas of words written, beginning
" with the moft fimple; the art of fpeak-
" ing is taken from the motion of his lips,

" his words being uttered *slowly* and *dis-*
" *tinctly:*—When I entered the room, and
" found myself surrounded with numbers
" of human forms, so oddly circumstanced, I
" felt a *sort of anxiety*, such as I might be sup-
" posed to feel had I been environed by an-
" other order of beings:—*I was soon relieved,*
" by being introduced to a most angelic
" young creature of about the age of *thir-*
" *teen.* She honored me with her new ac-
" quired conversation, but I may *truely* say,
" I could scarcely bear the power of her
" piercing eyes: she looked me through
" and through: she soon satisfied me that
" she was an apt scholar: she readily ap-
" prehended *all* I said, and *returned an-*
" *swers with the utmost facility.* She *read,*
" she *wrote* well. Her reading was *not* by
" rote. *She could cloath the same thoughts*
" *in a new set of words, and never vary*
" *from the original sense.* I have forgot
" the

APPENDIX.

" the book she took up, or the sentiments
" she made a new version of, but the effects
" were as follows:

VERSION.

" Lord Bacon has di-
" vided the whole of
" human knowledge,
" into *History — Poetry*
" — and *Philosophy*,
" which are referred to
" the *three* powers of
" Mind, *Memory — Ima-*
" *gination* — and *Rea-*
" *son* *.

" *A Nobleman* has
" parted the total of all
" Man's Study and Un-
" derstanding, into *an*
" *Account* of the Life,
" Manners, Religion,
" and Customs of *any*
" People or Country —
" *Verse* or Metre — *Mo-*
" *ral or Natural Know-*
" *ledge,* — which are
" pointed to the *three*
" Faculties of the *Soul*
" or Spirit: — the *Fa-*
" *culty of remembring —*
" *Thought* o. Concep-
" tion — and *Right*
" *Judgement.*

" I left *Mr. Braidwood*, and his pupils,
" with the satisfaction that *must result* from

---

* " This was read by *another* young lady, but that
" which I heard was *not less* difficult, nor less *faithfully*
" *translated.*" Pennant.

P 4

" a reflexion on *the utility of his art, and*
" *the merit of his labors*, who, after receiv-
" ing under his care, a being, that *seemed*
" to be merely endowed with a human
" form, could produce the *divina particula*
" *auræ* (*latent*, and, but for his skill,
" condemned to be *ever* latent in it); and
" *who could restore a child to its glad parents*,
" with a capacity of *exerting its rational*
" *powers*, by *expressing* sounds of duty,
" love, and affection."

 Pennant's Tour through Scotland, Vol.
  III. p. 256.

Copy

APPENDIX.

Copy of the *Form of Prayer*, taken from the mouth of the child (who *had been* dumb) mentioned in p. 150.

"O God! pardon all my sins, make *me* *good* and holy;—bless my *father* and my *sister*, and all my friends:—keep me from all evil, sin, and danger, and take my soul to heaven when I die, for Jesus Christ's sake! Amen!"

"A spe-

A *specimen* of the degree of perfection in written language, to which the naturally *deaf* are capable of arriving.

Written by a *deaf* pupil of Mr. Braidwood's without affiftance or amendment.

"On feeing GARRICK act.

"When Britain's *Rofcius* on the ftage ap-
"pears,
"Who charms all eyes, and *(I am told)*
"all *ears*,
"With eafe the various paffions I can trace,
"Clearly reflected from that wond'rous
"face;
"Whilft true conception, with juft action
"join'd,
"Strongly imprefs each image on my
"mind:—

What

"What need of sounds, when plainly I
 "descry
"Th' expressive features, and the speaking
 "eye?
"That eye, whose bright and penetrating
 "ray
"Doth *Shakespear's* meaning to my soul
 "convey:
"Best commentator on great Shakespear's
 "text!
"When *Garrick* acts, *no* passage seems per-
 "plext.
"C. S."

———

N.B. The above lines appeared in some of the London News-papers and Magazines of the time, viz. about the end of the year 1768.

SKETCH

SKETCH

OF

A Plan for Perpetuating, and Extending the Benefits of the beforementioned important Art.

FIRST,

THAT (in imitation of the gracious example of HIS MAJESTY) a subscription be opened, for the purpose of providing a fund for a public charitable institution.

SECONDLY,

That the sum so subscribed be lodged in the hands of respectable bankers, or others, in the different parts of these kingdoms, until

until called for by order of the governor and directors.

THIRDLY,

That a Governor be nominated by HIS MAJESTY, and a number of Directors chosen by the Subscribers, for the management of this stock;

FOURTHLY,

That when a sum sufficient for the execution of this Plan shall be raised, the Governor and Directors shall immediately take the most effectual measures for establishing a *public Academy* for the purposes herein specified.

FIFTHLY,

APPENDIX.

FIFTHLY,

That, in order to prevent the interest from being mismanaged, or becoming a sinecure, no part of the fund to be applied but by written special order from the Governor.

SIXTHLY,

That no person be admitted to partake of the benefits of this establishment but such objects as, upon application, shall receive a special certificate of admission from the Governor and Directors.

SEVENTHLY,

That as soon as it shall appear that a sufficiency will be provided, such a number of ingenious young men as may be deemed necessary shall be qualified, and contracted with, without loss of time, as *Assistants*,

and

and *Succeſſors.*—And the benefits of this inſtitution ſhall be imparted to a certain number of young perſons *as ſoon as poſſible.*

FINIS.

www.ingramcontent.com/pod-product-compliance
Lightning Source LLC
Chambersburg PA
CBHW021805230426
43669CB00008B/636